"The man who beats the drum does not know how far the sound goes."
— African proverb.

What does God know about business? Making the right decisions in tough times is a credible, profound and inspiring testimony of a successful businessman's conversion and his steadfast determination and focused progression towards a closer walk with God. Written with a refreshing emotional and intellectual honesty, and with the linguistic clarity and appeal only possible in the total absence of any motive other than simply sharing the almost incomprehensible grace of a deep relationship with Jesus Christ, this is a book for Christians and non-Christians alike.

This practical guide is an autobiographical account of how the author's focused obedience brought a real understanding of a life filled with God's presence, not only to himself but also to his family, colleagues, business associates, friends and countless others. This practical guide provides valuable keys to uncovering great biblical truths, which in turn will culminate in a truly meaningful life.

May God enhance the sound of this testimony in the life of every reader. *— Francois van Niekerk, Chairman of Atterbury Investment Holdings*

I read your book in two sittings (something I rarely do with my busy schedule) and was totally enthralled. The book was very engaging and the stories of God's faithfulness in your everyday walk made me long for the kind of intimacy I had with the Lord when I was a young man. I realized that I had lost some of the sense of expectation and excitement for what He had for me each day and your book has helped me recapture that. *— Jeff Behan, CEO, Vision Trust Communications USA*

What does God know about business? gave me encouragement to be faithful to trust and honour HIM in our dealings in business, fellowship, family, and church. It was refreshing to hear of real life examples of HIS work in all aspects of our lives, when we are faithful to seek HIM each and every day with the expectation that HE will speak to us and does care for our concerns. For this I am eternally grateful to you in writing this book and giving me a boost of encouragement to know HE loves and cares for ME. – *Staffard Belaire, USA*

Nico van der Merwe, a successful Christian businessman, repacks a clear solution for our existential problems and that is: God knows; God has the answer to our life's vacuums and He can fill it. With his personal experience of God he articulates the four pillars of Christianity, namely morality, honesty, compassion and commitment and their marvelous outcomes... In this book he comes up with the wonderful results of being a disciple of God in every corner of life – a life lived in the Coram Deo, in the presence of God. This book is a magnum opus for tough times in any component of life. – *Prof Kobus de Smidt, Head of the Department of New Testament, Auckland Park Theological Seminary*

I don't like to read. I battle to complete things and usually give up. I battle with self-discipline and I am not a good leader for my family. When I picked up your book I could not put it down. The Lord showed me the sin in my life – I am materialistic; I don't have self-discipline; I lust; I don't trust Him. I steal from Him by not giving Him my 'first fruits'. I have immediately started getting up at 05:00 and keeping my quiet time. It was a fantastic way to start the day. – *MM, Pretoria*

Thank you for a very inspiring book. It opened my eyes. I have always wondered why I did not experience a deeper relationship with God. Your book clearly spelled it out – I did not spend enough time with Him and I did not submit and trust Him fully. My eyes have opened for the first time and I experience big changes on all levels of my life. I never thought it was possible to get addicted to God! – *Flip, SA*

The question "How does one hear the voice of God?" has always been an issue I never clearly understood. I could never understand how people could say "I heard the Lord's voice on a specific issue in my life". I have asked many people over many years how do you talk to God and how does God talk to me. Nobody has made it as clear as in this book. I have had times in my life that I have been seeking for answers from the Bible without receiving them and I felt as if my prayers only went to the ceiling! The result was that I started seeking the Bible less and less and my quiet times eventually stopped to exist.

What does God know about Business? has totally changed my whole view on spirituality!! For the first time I understand the concept of 'quiet time'. The fact that the author shared in simple terms what the Lord has meant for him personally and in his business is the success recipe of the book. I could immediately relate to the content and I am sure it is going to change a lot of people's lives , as it changed mine! – *Johan, SA*

I had to write immediately! Thank you for writing such an inspirational testimony which relates to most of us! I thoroughly enjoyed your book and couldn't put it down! I am a committed Christian and attend a church in PMB called the "All Saints United Church" and also run the church services for a retirement village here. However, there was a lot to learn from your book *What does God know about business?* Congratulations on all your achievements despite difficult circumstances at times. Your story was interesting to say the least. God spoke to ME as well, while I read it - I just feel a certain peace now. *— Pam, KZN, SA*

I think the book is brilliant. It is written with a lot of honesty and everybody can benefit from it — not just business people. It made me think and the Lord used it to speak to me in my own personal problems. *— PvdW, SA*

I received the book from a colleague. I have not read something so practical in a long time. *— Chris, SA*

Thank you for a fantastic book. I have made a lot of wrong choices the past two years and I am still battling with the effects. The Lord has spoken to me through this book and I praise the Lord that this book came into my possession which I read with so much emotion. *— Leon, SA*

WHAT DOES GOD KNOW ABOUT BUSINESS?

Making the right decisions in tough times

A personal testimony

NICO VAN DER MERWE

First published in South Africa by Puisano Business Development Group (Pty) Ltd, Puisano Place, P. O. Box 63, Wapadrand, South Africa, 0050.

www.puisano.com

International Standard Book Number: 9781453842980

Editor: Connie Nel

Book design: Rudi Sadler, Puisano Business Development Group (Pty) Ltd

Front cover photograph: Kevin Pohl

Printed and bound in South Africa by Business Print

To order: www.godandbusiness.co.za

To view the Eduplex, visit www.maps.google.com

Pre-school	Primary School
1183 Dormer Avenue	1192 Cowgill Street
Queenswood	Queenswood
Pretoria, Gauteng	Pretoria, Gauteng
South Africa	South Africa

DEDICATION

This testimony of the Lord's grace in my life is dedicated to my wife, children and grandchildren.

Anita
No man could ask for a better wife, friend, lover and business partner.

Pieta
Our dedicated, gentle giant of a son-in-law.
Louise
Our strong, principle-centered daughter.
Zander and Kelvin
The two best behaved and loving grandchildren on earth.

Nico Junior
Our son with the best of both of us. May you never lose your sense of humor.
Lize
A loving wife, mother and daughter-in-law.
Nico IV
Our strong-willed grandson.
Lara
Our angel of a granddaughter.

You are all a wonderful blessing to me.

ACKNOWLEDGEMENTS

I would like to thank the many people throughout the world who have built into my life over many years through their prayers, reprimands, motivation and friendship. The support I received from Colla Kruger, Fanus van Zyl and Johan Pretorius—every Thursday morning for the past 20 years—has carried me through both good and bad times. You will never know how much your fellowship and honest advice have meant to me, often putting life's trials and tribulations into the right perspective.

Thank you to Francois van Niekerk for his friendship and encouragement to complete this testimony and for his kind words on the back cover of this publication.

Thank you to Prof. Dion du Plessis for checking the facts in the chapter on "Burnout". You have been a good friend over many years and have also witnessed God's immeasurable grace in my life.

What can I say about my best friend, Gerrit Wolfaardt? Very few people have the privilege of such a close friendship. Over the years, we have laughed and cried together as we realized how similar our life stories were and how God's loving mercy manifested itself in our lives. Thank you for your inspiration, advice, input and time dedicated to this book. You are a true friend.

I would like to thank Anita for her love, support and honesty. Thank you for the balance that you have brought into my life. Without you by my side, many of the miracles shared in this book would not have taken place.

A word of thanks to my editor, Connie Nel, for the many hours of hard work editing an Afrikaans-speaking author's English, and finally, to Dawid Pieterse from Puisano, my heartfelt thanks for his contribution in getting my book published.

To all of you, I owe my sincere gratitude.

Nico

CONTENTS

FOREWORD

I have known Nico for 33 years and we have become the very best of friends. His account of redemption and obedience is authentic and powerful, yet simple. Therein lies its great power to motivate and assist other Christians and seekers to embark on an intimate journey with God. If you have never encountered God in a personal way, this book will inspire you to hunger and seek after a closer relationship with Him.

As a Bible teacher in many countries around the world over the last 20 years, I have become most concerned with the manner in which people apply the truths contained in the Scriptures to their daily lives. One may learn how to interpret and understand the Bible, but how do you transfer it from the "head" to the "heart", from intellectual assent to life-changing reality? This book will provide invaluable guidelines if you choose to follow the steps that the author implemented in his own life.

Nico's experiences as a businessman in South Africa are backed up with testimony upon testimony of God's faithfulness in his business and his personal life. The radical results it produced will inspire you and increase your faith.

In brief, it all boils down to his quiet time with God every morning. This is when Nico prays, seeks guidance and grapples with God over everything that affects his life. I have been involved in this journey and have experienced first-hand the miraculous growth of his business. Moreover, I have learnt from him what it means to have a truly intimate relationship with God.

We live in an age of information overload and have become too busy and impatient to seek God's will and to wait upon Him for guidance, whether in our personal lives or our professional pursuits. We neglect Him to our own detriment and peril. Should we continue down this road, it will eventually lead to a stagnant spiritual life with no testimony of any worth.

This book will inspire and encourage you to embark on a vibrant walk with God, which in turn will lead to spiritual transformation at the deepest level. It is impossible to enjoy such an intimate time with God on a daily basis without it affecting your daily walk and encouraging a life of holiness—not a set of rules to live by, but a hunger and thirst to become more like Jesus. And when your own life is impacted in this manner, you will begin to impact the world around you for the better.

If you are tired of spiritual mediocrity, or if you need a fresh breeze of inspiration to regain, or perhaps for the first time enter into a close and life-changing relationship with your Heavenly Father, read on.

I pray that God will reveal Himself to you in a powerful way as you set off on this spiritual journey.

The Rev. Gerrit J. Wolfaardt

Associate Pastor
International Anglican Church, Colorado Springs, CO 80919, USA
Executive Director, The Word For All Nations, Colorado Springs

CHAPTER 1

INTRODUCTION

"I am with you. Do not fear.
Never doubt My love and power.
Your heights of success will be won by the
daily persistent doing of what I have said …

Never falter, go forward so boldly,
so unafraid.
I am beside you to help
and strengthen you …

Say 'All is well' to everything. 'All is well'." [1]

(Ed. A.J. Russell)

"Heee-haaa!" my best friend Gerrit yelled as he plunged into the pool, following the stripper.

It was New Year's Eve, 1977, and a balmy summer's evening. We used to have the best year-end parties in town with a lamb on the spit, draft beer, wine, music and dancing until the early hours of the morning. We were known for these parties among our friends and their friends, many of whom we only saw once a year.

As the stripper started her act on our patio table, I watched the faces of my friends, eagerly awaiting the next piece of clothing to fly. Their wives' faces, though, reflected utter dismay as they looked at their husbands. But, something new had to be devised for these parties every year—and the stripper seemed a good idea for this one.

I stood to one side and watched the spectacle unfolding. And then, as if from nowhere, I heard a voice, "Tonight, you have gone too far." I looked around, but there was no-one close by and I shrugged it off as my imagination … but the remark lingered in my mind until I finally began to ponder my life and ways as a young man.

What I am about to share is an account of my life as a businessman in South Africa. And I will be the first to add that I am an ordinary man with many faults—a man on whom God took pity.

Thank you for allowing me to share my walk with the Lord with you. You will come to know how He guided me, reprimanded me, how He provided in miraculous ways, and the priceless lessons He taught me as a businessman. However, this book is not only about me. It also highlights the importance of having a God-given vision and finding the key to a fulfilling relationship with God.

This is a personal testimony and not intended to be a formula for success—far from it. It is the story of my imperfect life and my imperfect walk with God. May this book be a blessing to all who read it, and above all, may it turn the reader's eyes to Him who is omnipotent and wholly engaged in our everyday lives.

The Early Years ...

I clearly remember accompanying a friend to a swimming club event in my fourth year at school and being invited to participate in the club championships that evening. I was entered for the under-nine 25-yard freestyle event. I came second and ran all the way home to show my dad the accolade—my first trophy ever.

This little trophy initiated my career as a sportsman. At 18, I was selected to represent South Africa in the very last swimming tour to Europe, before the anti-apartheid sports boycott prevented all South African sports teams from competing internationally. That year (1969), I managed to attain the world's fifth fastest time in the 100-meter freestyle event.

Despite these achievements, I hated school, hated university and, most of all, hated living at home. My dad was an alcoholic, and the constant stress and conflict caused me to become tense and aggressive.

I met my wife Anita, a pharmacist, while completing my two-year practical training as part of my pharmaceutical degree. I was only 21, but we decided to get married before returning to the town of Potchefstroom where I attended university. Anita worked as a pharmacist in the local government hospital, while I completed my five-year course.

One morning, during my penultimate year at university, I received a distressing phone call from the police informing me that my dad had shot my mother and unsuccessfully tried to commit suicide. I was devastated. During the seemingly endless trip to Pretoria, I begged God to spare my parents. On arrival, I was told that my mother had died as a result of her injuries and that my father was in intensive care. He eventually recovered and, after spending some time in a psychiatric hospital and later in a retirement home, passed away at the age of 83.*

---

* Some years before my father's death, the Lord impressed upon my heart to forgive him for what he had done. This turned out to be more difficult than anticipated, as I realized that I had been harboring this unforgiveness towards him for many, many years. One morning, during my quiet time, I finally managed to verbalize my forgiveness, and the next time I saw him, I simply said, "Dad, I want you to know that I love you very much." I will never forget the look in his eyes as he thanked me. It was a great relief to finally put this traumatic event behind me.

Immediately after my mother's funeral, I returned to Potchefstroom to complete my studies. Little did I realize that God was trying to attract my attention … that as young as I was, I was ultimately on the same track as my dad.

After obtaining my degree, Anita and I borrowed money and bought our own pharmacy. To supplement our income, I got into the habit of working in an emergency pharmacy for seven days a week, up to eleven o'clock at night. At that time, we already had two lovely children, Louise and Nico Junior, whom I only saw when Anita brought my lunch to the pharmacy on Sundays.

I worked hard and played hard (as the New Year's Eve parties testified), but my conscience gradually steered me in a different direction. God had a plan for my life …

An Appointment with God

After six years of working day and night, I considered attending our local church on the odd free Sunday. The church had a new young pastor, whom we later befriended. We invited the pastoral couple to dinner one evening and he impressed me with his wisdom and insight. I accepted his invitation to join a small group of people for a prayer meeting on the following Saturday morning.

The meeting was attended by six people only: the pastor, four ladies and me. We sat in a tiny office discussing various topics and then prayed about them. I was so nervous I could not pray out loud, let alone to Someone I hardly even knew!

What really struck me was the sincerity of every single person in that little group. Listening to their prayers, I realized that they actually knew the Deity to whom they were praying; and it certainly appeared as though they had some kind of personal relationship with God. I intuitively knew that they had something I did not have … and I desperately wanted to share in this.

I knew that God's Word had something to do with this relationship. Yet, whenever I read the Bible I could not understand why people raved about it, as it did not make any sense to me. It was literally a closed book. After the second or third prayer meeting, I plucked up the necessary courage to pray by mumbling a few words. I clearly remember my head spinning uncontrollably, as if in a tumble-dryer.

Anita and I started attending church quite regularly. One Sunday evening, our pastor mentioned that many people wished to accept Christ into their lives, but that they felt like 14-year olds standing in the passage—no longer children, nor as yet adults. He invited members of the congregation to stand up if they were intent on committing or even re-committing their lives to the Lord, rather than remaining in "the passage". That evening, Anita and I stood up for the first time and committed our lives to Jesus Christ.

The year was 1980 and life would never be the same again ...

Quiet Time – Spending Time Alone with God

Our pastor encouraged us to "delve into the Word". I took this to heart and rose at five every morning to pray and read the Bible. I met a friend at one of the Saturday prayer meetings and we started comparing notes on what we felt the Lord was telling us in our quiet time. It was amazing how often the messages were similar, even though we read from different parts of the Bible. This greatly encouraged us, as the Bible became more meaningful. I marveled at the way in which the Holy Spirit started revealing the Word to me.

Soon after my conversion, I had three significant encounters which convinced me that this was a serious matter. These experiences had a profound impact on my thoughts as a Christian and shaped the way I was to think about God ... even in my business.

The first experience pertained to a question posed by a friend as to whether Jesus actually rose from the dead. "How do you know for sure?" he asked. I replied, "Because the Bible tells us so. In fact, at one stage Jesus appeared to 500 people after His resurrection."

My friend responded, "Show me."

As a relatively inexperienced Christian, I had no idea where to start looking for this particular Scripture. As I walked to our bedroom to fetch my Bible, I quickly said a short prayer asking the Lord to please help me, not for His sake but for mine, as I felt my reputation was at stake!

I walked into the room, picked up the Bible and opened it, fervently looking for the passage. My eyes fell on the following verses: "I passed on to you right from the first what had been told to me, that Christ died for our sins just as the Scriptures said he would, and that he was buried, and that three days afterwards he arose from the grave just as the prophets foretold. He was seen by Peter and later by the rest of 'the Twelve'. After that he was seen by more than five hundred Christian brothers at one time, most of whom are still alive, though some have died by now" (I Corinthians 15:3–6).

I literally froze, realizing that this was no coincidence. This was not some fluke, but our living God helping me in my ignorance, whilst my reputation was on the line.

This proved to be a turning point in my life. For the first time, the Lord provided me with a direct answer from His Word. I intuitively realized that I could trust His Word. All that remained for me to do was to seek the Lord's face, study and meditate on His Word, and its meaning and depth would be revealed to me by the Holy Spirit.

Soon after this incident, I made another request known to the Lord. We were urgently seeking a pharmacist for one of our pharmacies. During my quiet time one morning, I asked the Lord to please send me a pharmacist. I added that it was an emergency and that I needed to find a manager before twelve noon!

At eleven o'clock, I received a phone call from the wife of a local pastor, enquiring whether we by any chance had a position available for a pharmacist. Again, I was utterly amazed and could hardly believe God's goodness in providing that which I had asked of Him just a few hours earlier.

Soon afterwards, I asked God to reveal to me whether we should continue with the second pharmacy we had purchased, or rather consider closing the business. Three days later, our accountant phoned and informed me that preliminary calculations indicated that the second business had made a substantial loss. I immediately took this as the Lord's confirmation that we should close it down and incorporate it into our first pharmacy, just further down the road. A couple of months later, final audited figures revealed that we had actually made a small profit, but by then the second pharmacy had already been closed.

The lessons learnt through these three experiences were: firstly, that you may seek the Lord's help and guidance; secondly, that He does intervene when you ask according to His will; and thirdly, that He often uses circumstances or people to steer us in the right direction. More about this later ...

CHAPTER 2

MAKING THE RIGHT DECISIONS

"If you want favor with both God and man,
and a reputation for good judgment
and common sense,
then trust the Lord completely;
don't ever trust yourself.
In everything you do, put God first,
and he will direct you
and crown your efforts with success."

(Proverbs 3:4–6)

Let me be frank: trusting God in every single business deal is not always easy. Being human, I often still overstep the mark by wanting to follow my own instincts. After all, I have a God-given talent! But, I had to learn the hard way as projects, initiated of my own accord, struggled to get off the ground.

Yet, God remained faithful as I continued to seek His will.

Anita and I bought our first home in Pretoria in 1975. A 25% deposit was required and I "dipped" into our company's overdraft facility to settle this amount. We obtained financing over 20 years, and although we have made a few alterations as our circumstances changed over the years, we still live in the same house, 35 years later.

In 1985, we were appointed as general agents for a Swiss hearing-aid company. Soon after my training in the repair of hearing aids at the factory in Switzerland, I also received training at a German earmold laboratory. At the same time, we recruited our first six agents and flew them to Switzerland for training, as there was no formal training available for hearing-aid acousticians in our country at the time.

In the meantime, I converted the pharmacy's small kitchen into a laboratory. I distinctly remember manufacturing my first 10 earmolds for our agents on 1 January 1986. It was a daunting, but exhilarating experience. Although I was aware of the Lord's blessing on this venture, it was a rather lonely time as I had no company apart from the pharmacy staff who had to attend to their own responsibilities.

For the first six months, I manufactured earmolds in the morning, saw my own patients in the afternoon and serviced any defective hearing aids during the evening. Fortunately, there were not that many, as we had just started out and all the products were new. After six months, I appointed our first laboratory technician to assist with the manufacturing of earmolds. At a prayer meeting one morning, a friend mentioned that he had come across an unemployed Dutchman living in a garage. I was extremely moved by this account and decided to employ this homeless person as our first laboratory technician. He, in turn, trained the first deaf person we employed to manufacture earmolds.

From very small beginnings, the Lord blessed the business and soon we had another group of 12 agents trained in Switzerland.

I faithfully kept seeking the Lord's guidance with regard to important business decisions, and He rewarded my obedience by performing one miracle after another in my life.

Miracle One: Deciding on a Holiday Home

In December 1988, our family went on vacation to one of the most beautiful spots in the world, a fishing village called Hermanus, located between mountains and the sea, approximately one and a half hours' drive from Cape Town. 1,000 miles away from Pretoria, we found the roads in those days to be good and the traffic slight, resulting in a day-long journey.

Along with some friends, we rented a holiday home in Vermont, approximately four miles to the west of Hermanus. Anita and I thought it would be a privilege to have a holiday home in the Cape in order to enjoy the warm summer days and cool Atlantic sea breeze at night. During winter, Hermanus is also a wonderful spot for watching Southern Right whales frolicking in the bay.

I suggested we seek the Lord's guidance for acquiring a holiday home. Despite having separate quiet times, that morning both Anita and I received the same Scripture: "If I ride the morning winds to the farthest oceans, even there your hand will guide me, your strength will support me" (Psalm 139:9–10).

To us, this was a clear sign of God's blessing to continue. We called on an estate agent to enquire about available properties. I mentioned that we were from Pretoria, far from the ocean, and that we would prefer a house as close as possible to the sea. He had only one stand to show us, available at approximately US$60,000. The property was surrounded by a sand dune to the rear, a nature conservancy on three sides and a magnificent sea view. Although this was very expensive for a plot of land at the time, we decided to buy.

Despite our initial certainty, I experienced an inexplicable unease about this decision. We were very happy with the property, but for some reason

I couldn't shake the prevailing discomfort. I returned to the estate agent and mentioned this to him. He looked at me for a moment, jumped up and walked to the map on the wall where the various stands for sale were displayed. He could barely suppress his excitement when he turned to me and said, "Nico, I forgot to mention that the stand you bought is one of only two stands in this whole area which can be subdivided."

We followed his advice and subdivided the stand. The back section, literally a sand dune, was sold for exactly the same amount we had paid for the entire property. Some would call it "a good business deal" or a "stroke of luck", but we knew that this was a gift from God—a miracle.

Had anyone told me at the time, "If you pray and ask the Lord, He will give you the best property in the region for free," I would not have believed it possible. Yet, God provided once again. We built a comfortable home and called it "Back to Basics". This is where our family gathers every December to relax and recharge our batteries for the year ahead. Visitors from around the world can testify to the peace and serenity they have experienced when sharing in this gift from God.

Miracle Two: Deciding on a Company Building

The Lord continued to bless our company, and our pharmacy soon ran out of space. It was time to scout for larger premises to accommodate our wholesale division, the administration, as well as the earmold and service laboratories.

In 1989, we considered refurbishing a residential house diagonally across from the pharmacy. The owner refused our offer, saying, "I know I will regret your fantastic offer, but for some reason I feel I cannot accept." I was extremely disappointed, but continued to pray.

Soon thereafter, I saw a tiny advertisement in a local newspaper (which I never read) relating to a new building for sale next to a retirement village. I knew the building well, as Anita's mom lived next-door. I approached the owner while he was constructing the 6,000 sq. ft. building and asked whether he would be interested in selling. At the time, he was intent on letting the premises and declined.

I called the estate agent and expressed interest in purchasing the building. On the following Monday, I went and showed the building to my friend Gerrit and an architect friend, and asked them whether they considered it good value for money. They jokingly said that the price was so low, there had to be something wrong! Although the price was fair, I had doubts about expanding to such an extent. We only required slightly larger premises, not a whole building!

I decided that unless the Lord gave us clear direction, I would not buy this property. Moreover, we were about to leave for a winter camping holiday in Botswana on the Friday. How would it be possible for the Lord to answer me in such a short period of time and, beyond that, to get the necessary documents drafted and signed?

On the Wednesday morning at four o'clock, I had my quiet time and asked the Lord for guidance. I still recall saying, "Lord, I am sorry to put You under such pressure, but I really need to know today what to do about the building, as we are leaving for Botswana on Friday. Please show me Your will."

At that stage, I was working my way through the *One Year Bible* and the passage I had to read that morning was 2 Kings 6: "One day the seminary students came to Elisha and told him, 'As you can see, our dormitory is too small. Tell us, as our president, whether we can build a new one down beside the Jordan River, where there are plenty of logs.' 'All right,' he told them, 'go ahead.' 'Please, sir, come with us,' someone suggested. 'I will,' he said" (2 Kings 6:1–3).

I was dumbstruck. Doubt immediately set in. This was not possible! So quickly! It just had to be a coincidence.

When I shared this with my family over breakfast, my daughter Louise said, "Wow, Dad, isn't the Lord amazing!" That was all the confirmation I needed. We left for Botswana on the Friday and all the paperwork was signed and sealed.

God provided a new home for our company and the building was officially opened by the Secretary of Health in March 1990. That evening, the heavens opened up and it rained like seldom before. Africans believe that if it rains when you celebrate a special occasion, it is a sign of the Lord's blessing. Indeed it was.

I had a brass plaque made with 2 Kings 6:1–3 engraved on it and mounted it on one of the walls in the reception area. One of my staff members asked why I didn't display it in a more prominent place where our visitors could see it. I explained that the plaque was there to remind me of God's greatness and that our clients most probably wouldn't understand the significance of that particular extract from the Bible. It would also serve as a reminder when things got tough, that God was involved in the decision to purchase the building, and that He would be with us always, just as He had promised.

Two years later, I had to stand in front of the same plaque and remind myself that the Lord had indeed blessed the purchase of this building, that He was there with us and that we needed to persevere through the very difficult period we experienced at the time.

Miracle Three: Deciding on Expansion

In 1993, a year before the first democratic election and the abolition of apartheid, the general mood in our country was very negative. This resulted in riots, bombings and killings, with the police trying their best to keep law and order. Those were dark days in the history of South Africa.

Running a business during this period was challenging, to say the least. One weekend, a Kenyan missionary stayed over in our home and I shared with him that we wished to expand into Africa. During the apartheid years we never deemed ourselves part of Africa and whenever we spoke about "Africa", we generally referred to countries beyond the borders of South Africa.

I told him about the negative atmosphere in our country and the prevailing "let's wait and see" attitude. The last thing on anybody's mind was to expand—we had to maintain the status quo. People were emigrating, not expanding!

We prayed together, seeking God's guidance for the current circumstances and what the future would hold for us, by no means expecting the Lord to provide an answer from Isaiah: "Enlarge the place of your tent, stretch your tent curtains wide, do not hold back; lengthen your cords, strengthen your stakes. For you will spread out to the right and to the left; ... Do not be afraid; you will not suffer shame. Do not fear disgrace; you will not be humiliated ... For your Maker is your husband—the LORD Almighty is his name ..." (Isaiah 54:2–5 NIV).

The Lord taught me an amazing lesson: When times are really tough and the stakes are down, He leads His children to go against the tide by moving in the Spirit to the contrary. When people are leaving, He says, "Stay!" When people are disinvesting, He says, "Invest!" When people are selling, He says, "Buy!" When there is fear, He says, "Have faith!"

It was quite evident that if the Lord intimated that we were about to burst at the seams, we would need more space.

The property developer, from whom I bought our first building, developed two similar buildings right next to our property. I got in touch with him and offered to purchase the small building right next to ours. He was adamant, "No, you must buy everything (two buildings plus a vacant lot next to the last building), or nothing. I know I will regret selling these properties, but one never knows what the future will hold after the election."

I made him an offer and we bought not only double what we thought we would need, but also a plot of land adjacent to the last building for future expansion. The Lord clearly knew what was coming, but I had to deal with the fear and doubt in my own heart by stepping out in faith and obedience to His guidance.

By the time the first democratically elected government came into power, we had already let most of the extra floor space. But soon thereafter, our business started expanding to the point where we occupied all three buildings within a few years.

Miracle Four: Deciding on a Property for Our School

In the meantime, God gave me a vision to make a difference in education for deaf children. In 1992, we established the Foundation for Children with a Hearing Loss in Southern Africa in pursuit of God's vision. It was my intention to build the school on the small vacant plot (approximately 10,000 sq. ft.) next to our existing premises. I reasoned that, after all, children in Europe did not have playgrounds or sports fields and that this plot would be ideal in size.

Unbeknown to me, I was limiting God's vision. I am very conservative by nature and over the years the Lord has had a hard time convincing me that I should trust Him and dream big.

The cost of erecting a four-storey school on this small area of land was prohibitive. We had a look at another 50,000 sq. ft. property not far from our offices, but the location was not ideal, mainly due to the traffic noise. In addition, the owner rejected our offer of US$100,000. While searching for the right property, I visited our Swiss donors to finalize their donation and to obtain their commitment to finance the pre-school.

While in Zurich, I received a call from one of my senior managers informing me that he had discovered a 240,000 sq. ft. vacant plot, two blocks away from our offices, which would be ideal for a school. And, the price was less than US$100,000! Even in our country the asking price was ridiculously low, as the value was 20 times higher. This was unbelievable, but we immediately took an option on the land pending my arrival back in South Africa.

Sleep evaded me that night and I started making endless plans. Why such a large expanse, 24 times bigger than originally planned for the building? Surely, this must be a fantastic business opportunity! If I bought the property, subdivided it and then sold half to our Foundation, it would benefit both our family and the Foundation. This could only have been from God.

On-and-on my mind raced, until I had my quiet time. I was elated and ready to praise the Lord for His goodness, His provision and His faithfulness. I had scheduled a meeting with the donors the following morning, and needed to ask the Lord for His guidance and blessing. I was about to learn a lesson never to be forgotten.

My devotional reading was from C.H. Spurgeon's *Cheque Book of the Bank of Faith*. He starts by quoting Proverbs 10:9: "He that walketh uprightly walketh surely," and then continues, "His walk may be slow, but it is sure. He that hasteth to be rich shall not be innocent nor sure; but steady perseverance in integrity, if it does not bring riches, will certainly bring peace. In doing that which is just and right we are like one walking upon a rock, for we have confidence that every step we take is upon solid and safe ground. On the other hand, the utmost success through questionable transactions must always be hollow and treacherous, and the man who has gained it must always be afraid that a day of reckoning will come, and then his gains will condemn him." [1]

This reminded me of the biblical account of Achan who took a beautiful Babylonian garment, as well as some silver and gold from the enemy in violation of God's command to destroy everything, except that which was reserved for the Lord's treasury. The stolen goods were laid on the ground in front of Joshua, and Achan's gains ultimately resulted in the demise of the entire family, his livestock and all that he possessed (Joshua 7).

I begged the Lord's forgiveness for my selfishness and the greed in my own heart, and I thanked Him for exposing my sinful thoughts, thus showing me the right way. What a valuable lesson—and what a wonderful and amazing God we have.

Deciding on Other Investments

Our family invested in other properties as well, mainly to accommodate our Ear Institute branches throughout the country and to counteract the high rental and annual rent escalation (between 10% and 12% per annum). We usually pray before purchasing any property, seeking God's will and asking Him to close the doors should He not want us to continue with the transaction, whatever the reason may be.

I am ever mindful *not* to build a kingdom here on earth, but rather in heaven. Over the years, I have learnt that the only way to do so is not to over-extend, but to maintain a balance between expanding a business and being generous towards the church and those in need; be it staff, family, friends or the poor.

We often felt guided to purchase some properties, which at times seemed to be an odd notion. All that remained was to go back to the Word knowing that we had prayed about it—often for years. Whatever the outcome, it was not for us to question, but only to accept. Only God knows what the future holds.

Time after time, Jeremiah 29:5–7 cropped up as we planned expansion: "Build homes and plan to stay; plant vineyards, for you will be there many years. Marry and have children, and then find mates for them and have many grandchildren. Multiply! Don't dwindle away! And work for the peace and prosperity of Babylon. Pray for her, for if Babylon has peace, so will you."

This was especially relevant in those times when many white South Africans left for Australia, Europe and the USA, seeking safety, security, better opportunities and a more lucrative future for their children.

As we invested and operated our business during difficult conditions, Jeremiah 29:11–14 sustained me no end: "For I know the plans I have for you, says the Lord. They are plans for good and not for evil, to give you a future and a hope. In those days when you pray, I will listen. You will find me when you seek me, if you look for me in earnest. Yes, says the Lord, I will be found by you ..."

As you read about the amazing ways in which the Lord had led me with the purchasing of properties, I trust that you will realize that I am no-one special, but that there is something very special about the Lord. When you ask for guidance and He responds, you should listen and obey. He promised that we will find Him when we seek Him, if we look for Him in earnest. Take that promise and make it your own.

The secret is not to rush into making decisions. This is emphasized in one of my devotionals, God Calling: "Learn in the little daily things of life to delay action until you get My Guidance ... So many lives lack poise. For in the momentous decisions and the big things of life, they ask My help but into the small things they rush alone. By what you do in the small things those around you are most often antagonized or attracted." [2]

Verses 13 and 15 of Psalm 106 reaffirm man's tendency to rush into things: "Yet how quickly they forgot again! They wouldn't wait for him to act ... So he gave them their demands, but sent them leanness in their souls."

One has to be careful what to ask for when praying, as it may not be God's will. When we insist on our way rather than His way, it is possible that He may give us what we ask for, but the price to be paid may be "leanness in our souls". For me, this is much too high a price to pay. Always remember: "In his heart a man plans his course, but the LORD determines his steps" (Proverbs 16:9 NIV).

Deciding on a Business Offer

Some years ago, I received a phone call from the Vice President of a very large international company. He asked whether I would be interested in distributing their hearing aids in South Africa. At that stage, their products did not reach the potential that they would have liked to see.

I immediately showed interest and my ego was rather boosted. I shared the news with our management team, which included my wife Anita. I elaborated about the synergies, the increase in turnover and the wonderful possibilities. Anita wasn't impressed and she voiced her concern: "I don't agree. How do you teach these people new ways when they have rotten practices?" I was very upset, regarding it as a very negative response, and tried to persuade her otherwise.

The following morning, Anita and I prayed about the offer and asked the Lord whether this was from Him and whether we should pursue the proposal. The Holy Spirit prompted me to read Jeremiah 24:2–3: "I saw two baskets of figs placed in front of the Temple in Jerusalem. In one basket there were fresh, just-ripened figs, but in the other the figs were spoiled and moldy—too rotten to eat. Then the Lord said to me, 'What do you see, Jeremiah?' I replied, 'Figs, some very good and some very bad.'"

I asked the Lord what this Scripture meant. The response came to me in an instant. "You don't mix fresh and rotten figs," the exact words Anita used. I was stunned. Here was this huge company with the best advertisements, and the Lord intimated that they were nothing but rotten figs! Too hard to believe!

As I walked out of the house towards my car, Anita's words of the previous day, my own desires and the amazing way the Lord had led us that morning came to mind. I thought about a specific advertisement that the company ran, an advertisement I envied with all my heart, but as I reached out to open the car door, I clearly heard the Lord saying, "Nothing but rotten figs." A second message of caution ...

Notwithstanding, I decided to attend the meeting anyway just to see what was on the table, but fortunately, the day before the meeting, a management buy-out occurred. Since the offer, that company has had a number of management changes and limited success.

The Role of Other People in Decision-making

In a number of instances, the Lord also used other people to steer me in the right direction, only to have them withdraw at the last minute so that we could continue on our own. I am very grateful for these inputs, as I would probably not have made the decisions for fear of failure or lack of expertise.

On one occasion, we discussed the possibility of opening an Ear Institute in Cape Town in partnership with a local audiologist. She showed me a wonderful property surrounded by four hospitals. We acquired the property and built an Ear Institute. Two weeks prior to occupying the facility, her lawyers advised us of her withdrawal from our agreement. However, she was prepared to rent the facility from us.

We were very disappointed and decided to proceed with the business on our own, rather than take up her offer of renting the property. This was the best decision we could have made. Today, by the grace of God, the practice is a huge success. This experience taught me not to place my trust in people, but in the Lord only.

On another occasion, an audiologist working in a local school for the deaf paid us a visit and mentioned how inadequate their facilities were. At that stage, our international consultant, Dr. Morag Clark, was assisting the school by providing guidance in terms of their approach to education for the deaf.

I heard myself say, "Why don't we build a school?" and was shocked at my own words. The audiologist was ecstatic, and the idea of our own school was born in line with the vision the Lord had given me "to make a difference in deaf education". This lady would have been Head of our Parent Guidance section, but six months later she withdrew. The Lord clearly used her in directing me to follow His plans and vision for building a school.

At this point, I have to voice a word of caution. Some believers falsely assume that material possessions are a sign of God's spiritual blessing. This is a very dangerous trap, as I have seen many wealthy people become over-confident and complacent—forgetting the One who gave them riches in the first place. Deuteronomy 8:18 (NIV) reminds us, "But remember the LORD your God, for it is he who gives you the ability to produce wealth, and so confirms his covenant, which he swore to your forefathers, as it is today."

No matter how many homes I may own, how many properties I may acquire, or how much money I may make, I have *nothing* if I do not have a personal relationship with Jesus, acknowledging Him in all things.

Seek Him! Look for Him in earnest and you will not be disappointed, no matter what your circumstances may be. The Bible tells us to turn from our indifference and to "become enthusiastic about the things of God" (Revelation 3:19b).

CHAPTER 3

VISION

*"'Not by might, nor by power,
but by my Spirit,
says the Lord Almighty—you will succeed
because of my Spirit,
though you are few and weak.'"*

(Zechariah 4:6)

*"Do not despise this small beginning,
for the eyes of the Lord rejoice
to see the work begin ..."*

(Zechariah 4:10)

In his book, *The 8th Habit: From Effectiveness to Greatness*, Stephen R Covey, highly acclaimed author of *The Seven Habits of Highly Effective People*, says the following: "When you study the lives of all great achievers—those who have had the greatest influence on others, those who have made significant contributions, those who simply made things happen—you will find a pattern. Through their persistent efforts and inner struggle, they have greatly expanded their four native human intelligences or capacities. The highest manifestations of these four intelligences are: for the mental, *vision*; for the physical, *discipline*; for the emotional, *passion*; for the spiritual, *conscience*." [1]

Over the years, I have come to realize that some people have no vision, while others do not have the discipline or passion to pursue their vision, unless it is God-given.

In 1992, two years before the first democratic election in South Africa, our company sponsored the first national conference for Principals of schools for the deaf. For the first time, these leaders—from all ethnic groups—could mix freely and discuss issues of mutual concern. On my way to the conference, I caught a severe bout of flu.

While sitting in my hotel room, questioning the untimely illness, I experienced the Holy Spirit's soft voice urging me to read Jeremiah 29:11–12: "For I know the plans I have for you, says the Lord. They are plans for good and not for evil, to give you a future and a hope. In those days when you pray, I will listen. You will find me when you seek me, if you look for me in earnest."

Little did I know what a profound impact this Scripture would have on my future. It would continue to sustain me during very difficult times, especially when Anita was diagnosed with cancer.

A Vision from the Lord

During the Principals' conference, it became clear that traditional education for the deaf was in total disarray. I was motivated to become involved, although I didn't have the slightest idea how. I woke at four one morning and during my quiet time asked the Lord to show me what my potential contribution could be. I distinctly heard Him say, "I want you to make a difference in deaf education."

Five long years followed in which nothing seemed to happen. During this time, I established the Foundation for Children with a Hearing Loss in Southern Africa, spoke to numerous people and drafted endless documents. Gerrit and I even called on the World Bank in Washington DC, where I presented an outline of the vision behind the Foundation. Some people agreed, but others criticized the vision, accusing me of wanting to profit financially from the Foundation and its aims.

In 1997, we sold a few hearing aids (at cost price) to the remote island of Rodrigues, about 500 miles east of Mauritius. Shortly after they had paid for the hearing aids, they asked whether we could sponsor a plane ticket for a teacher, Dr. Morag Clark, who was advising them on the development of their program for deaf children. In addition, they said, she was willing to give lectures on a modern approach to the education of children with a hearing loss, to offset the costs.

I had no interest in paying for the ticket or organizing a conference for this teacher who was unknown to me. Our core business was audiology and not education! However, two days later I reluctantly agreed to pay for her ticket and to organize two conferences—one in Pretoria and one in Cape Town.

I was most surprised when more than 100 professionals enrolled for the Pretoria conference (which we had to divide into two sessions due to a lack of space) and 220 professionals for the Cape Town conference. The interest caught my attention and I started wondering who this woman was! In hindsight, it became clear that God was steering me in a different direction, despite my obvious lack of faith.

When I finally met Dr. Clark MBE (Member of the British Empire), I learnt that she was engaged in programs for the deaf in more than 10 countries. After the conferences, I asked her to read the Foundation document on her way to Rodrigues and to give me her honest opinion. Upon her return, she advised me to start with the professionals and not with the children.

"You want to begin at the wrong end, Nico," she said. "It is no good issuing children with hearing aids until you have trained professionals to use them in an educational setting. Today, with the help of modern hearing aids and cochlear implants, every deaf child can hear. Thanks to this modern technology, almost every deaf child can learn spoken language, provided they are exposed to nothing but normal, natural language."

She continued by introducing me to the "Natural Auditory Oral Approach" for educating deaf children. With this approach, they are able to acquire normal, spoken language without the use of sign language, thereby enabling them to attain their full potential with the necessary support.*

Small Beginnings

Finally, the penny dropped! I asked Dr. Clark whether she would assist me in following through on the vision of making a difference in education for the deaf, which the Lord had given me. She agreed, and four months later, in January 1998, we started training the first professionals in Pretoria. I was excited, but also a little disappointed that only eight people registered for the session. During my quiet time on the morning of the training, I read Zechariah 4:10: "Do not despise this small beginning, for the eyes of the Lord rejoice to see the work begin ..."

Then my eyes fell on verse 6: "'Not by might, nor by power, but by my Spirit, says the Lord Almighty—you will succeed because of my Spirit, though you are few and weak.'"

Six years after the Lord first called me to make a difference, the work finally commenced. It took me six years to learn that I was not to profit from this vision, but to invest my time, talent and treasure in what I believed the Lord had entrusted to me.

---

*The proviso is that deaf babies should be identified as early as possible after birth and fitted with the appropriate amplification. Joshinago Etano et al have shown that when this process happens within the first six months after birth, deaf babies have a 100% chance of acquiring normal spoken language.

Several professionals from various schools in our country received training, and after two years of work, Morag and I recognized the need to create our own facility. Instead of creating a special school for deaf children, we knew we needed to develop a mainstream school based on an inclusive model where we would cater for deaf children to learn alongside those with normal hearing. The school would also include a training facility for parents and professionals.

From the outset, we realized that in order to change education for the deaf, we would have to do more than just change the lives of a few children each year. We would have to train as many professionals as possible in our approach, and for that we needed a model in the form of a school where professionals could enjoy hands-on experience, as well as a training facility. This was the start of the miracle called "Eduplex" (Educational Complex).

I shared my vision with Swiss donors in 2000/01, and they generously sponsored the pre-school for 175 children with a small training facility for 25 people on the site which the Lord had miraculously provided.

In 2001, we began planning the buildings which were to accommodate deaf children in a mainstream setting. Special features included acoustically treated classrooms, small conversation rooms adjacent to each classroom, a parent guidance section, interactive gardens and a training facility with CCTV. Passionate people partnered with us by sharing their ideas and providing input, which allowed us to create something very special and unique for our children.

Turning Tragedy into Triumph

The Eduplex Pre-school was opened in March 2002 by South Africa's first black president, Mr. Nelson Mandela. In his opening address, he said that what we were doing here, was "turning tragedy into triumph". (Getting President Mandela to officially open the school was a miracle in itself!) Soon after the event, parents of the children with normal hearing asked when the Eduplex Primary School would follow. I was taken aback, as I was getting ready to move back into my comfort zone by first establishing the pre-school facility before venturing into something as ambitious as a primary school. However, the Lord had other plans.

At the time, we were doing some work for a Swiss Foundation at a school for the deaf in Harare, Zimbabwe. The Foundation's founder expressed interest in contributing to other projects, and I shared with him our primary school project. His Foundation generously offered to pay for the construction of the first six classrooms. However, with the input of our professional building consultants, we were eventually able to construct 10 classrooms with the money donated—thereby promising less and delivering more, a very important principle for me as a Christian.

Over the years, many people have visited our facilities. In fact, we implemented special tours on a monthly basis to accommodate the number of people wishing to visit the school. Visitors were truly amazed at what had been accomplished in such a short period of time. Moreover, we were able to provide employment to the unemployed parents of deaf children, thereby creating hope and a future for entire families.

This was in line with what the Lord promised me from Habakkuk 1:5 during the opening of the school in 2002: "The Lord replied: 'Look, and be amazed! You will be astounded at what I am about to do! For I am going to do something in your own lifetime that you will have to see to believe.'"

Funding the Final Phase

Having constructed the first 10 classrooms for the primary school, we set about planning the remainder of the facilities. One morning during my quiet time, I prayed about the school and the funding of the final phase. The Lord reminded me of a prominent Chief Executive Officer of an international company and a discussion we had regarding the financing of the school. My reading that morning was from Os Hillman's *Today God is First*. The author quotes 2 John 12 in which the apostle John says to his readers that he has much to write about, but that he hoped to rather visit them and talk face-to-face.

The devotional reading seemed to reaffirm the Scripture: "However, there are times when nothing but a face-to-face meeting is the appropriate means of communication." Hillman concludes, "Next time a situation arises that requires more focused communication, consider whether the situation requires a personal visit. You may find this will be the key to resolving issues that otherwise might end in stalemate." [2]

I knew at once that I had to go and see the Chief Executive Officer and discuss the financing of the school in person. I felt an urgency to phone him, but realized I had to time my call carefully—too early and he would be at home, too late and he would be in a meeting. I called him on his mobile number at quarter past eight (Swiss time) that morning. When he answered, I realized that he was probably in his car on the way to his office. His first words were, "This is perfect timing."

I explained that I wished to meet with him to discuss his company's possible financing of some classrooms. He replied, "This is an amazing coincidence!" He added that he was about to chair a pre-Board Planning Committee meeting to finalize the agenda for the following week's Board meeting. He suggested that I send him a three-page PowerPoint presentation outlining our needs before twelve noon. If accepted, they would present it to the Board for consideration.

One week later, I was informed that the Board had approved a donation of CHF1 million (roughly US$1 million), which would cover the construction of six classrooms. Had I not enjoyed my quiet time that morning during which I prayed about the financing, I would have missed the Lord's miraculous guidance and provision. We now had sufficient funds to start the construction of the final phase of Eduplex.

Construction by Faith

Shortly after the construction commenced in March 2006, other Swiss donors, who had promised the balance to complete the facilities, withdrew their support due to a local church using our facilities for adult Bible classes on Sundays. I had a choice: Ask the church to leave, or forfeit the money. Even though I explained that it was normal for churches and even political parties to use school premises in South Africa, as well as in the USA, the donors would not budge. I knew the Lord had hardened their hearts—and that He was about to do something miraculous once again.

Soon after the donors withdrew, the Foundation's Board was due to meet to decide whether the project should continue. During my quiet time on the morning of the meeting, the Lord instructed me very clearly from Zechariah 8:9 and 13b–15: "The Lord Almighty says: 'Get on with the job and finish it! You have been listening long enough! For since you began laying the foundation of the Temple, the prophets have been telling you about the blessings that await you when it's finished' ... 'So don't be afraid or discouraged! Get on with rebuilding the Temple! If you do, I will certainly bless you.'"

The Board decided to continue with the construction by faith. It was clear from the Lord's guidance that He expected my family to stand in the gap and accept the financial responsibility for the completion of the school, even though we did not have the financial means at that stage. In every which way, 2006 turned out to be one of the most difficult years I have ever experienced, but at the same time, one of the most spiritually fulfilling years.

On the same day after the Board meeting, I received an SMS from one of the parents at the school who was unaware of the donors' withdrawal, or the Board's decision to continue with the construction. She said the Lord had led her to send me the following Scripture: "So now, my son, may the Lord be with you and prosper you as you do what he told you to do and build the Temple of the Lord ... Be strong and courageous, fearless and enthusiastic! ... So get to work, and may the Lord be with you!" (1 Chronicles 22:11 and 16b).

During that time, I was reading *Man of Faith*[3], the amazing story of George Müller, which greatly encouraged me. Müller believed in a God who truly presented himself as "Father to the fatherless". Psalm 68:5 spoke to George Müller's heart in a unique way. Believing that his material needs would be supplied through faith and prayer only, Müller began a ministry for orphaned children in 1835.

Such total reliance on his Heavenly Father was nothing new for George Müller. Daily Bible reading and prayer formed an essential part of this prayer warrior's life. Within a few years, thousands of orphans in Ashley Down, near Bristol, England, had their needs met, and more, because of Müller's mission. Müller knew that the "Father of the fatherless" still provided for His children. He had God's Word for it.

People asked me whether I was concerned about the funds still required to complete the school. Like Müller, I felt clearly led not to go begging for money from anyone, but to trust the Lord to guide and provide—and to give my full attention to the construction of the final phase.

Obedience

At times, I felt despondent; yet, the Lord encouraged me in miraculous ways. In June 2006, Dr. Clark was holidaying in Scotland. She sent me an e-mail in which she expressed her shock about the withdrawal of the sponsors. After praying for the school, she felt compelled to send me the following Scripture: "'I know you well; you aren't strong, but you have tried to obey and have not denied my Name. Therefore I have opened a door to you that no one can shut'" (Revelation 3:8).

The next morning I received an e-mail from Gerrit (one of our Board members holidaying in Mexico) in which he also expressed his disappointment about the withdrawal of the promised donation. He went further by saying that the Lord laid it upon his heart for me to read ... Revelation 3:8! "'I know you well; you aren't strong, but you have tried to obey and have not denied my Name. Therefore I have opened a door to you that no one can shut.'"

I could hardly believe it. What tremendous encouragement! I continued my work with renewed strength and confidence, as per the Lord's instruction. After completing the facilities, I requested the architects to design a special area with two open doors that could not shut as a reminder of this amazing word the Lord gave—not only to me, but also to the staff, parents and children of the school.

Month-by-month, we literally had to trust the Lord to provide the necessary funds. It was a rather stressful and trying time for me. Our family decided to borrow US$2 million to complete the final phase and to cover some of the running costs. To obtain this loan, we had to put up our properties as collateral. This was a very difficult decision, but we clearly felt that this was what the Lord expected from us (standing in the gap), while trusting Him to provide in His own good time.

During my quiet time, around the middle of August that year, the Lord again encouraged me from I Chronicles 28:20: "'Be strong and courageous and get to work. Don't be frightened by the size of the task, for the Lord my God is with you; he will not forsake you. He will see to it that everything is finished correctly.'"

As I walked through the buildings, I noticed many features we had not planned for at the outset. However, these provided us with a much better facility. The sports commentators' box on the first floor and the large patio area downstairs near the new kitchen (ideal for a soft drink during our warm summer sports meetings) were some of these features, and I was again reminded that, "He will see to it that everything is finished correctly."

Like the oil multiplying in the jar of the widow (2 Kings 4:1–7), I can testify that the Lord provided the necessary funds every month—and even more than we needed for the construction bills. What makes this even more incredible is that, at the same time we were constructing the Eduplex's final phase, we also built our new Ear Institute facilities on the vacant plot next to our existing offices.

In addition, both projects received City Council approval during the same month, although we had been struggling to obtain approval for the construction of the Ear Institute for more than five years. I could only conclude that the Lord was testing my faith by placing an almost impossible situation before me. I had no choice, but to rely on Him completely … "'I know you well; you aren't strong, but you have tried to obey and have not denied my Name. Therefore I have opened a door to you that no one can shut'" (Revelation 3:8).

Comfort Zones

Prior to the commencement of the final construction phase, I was on a flight from the Middle East, reading *The Dream Giver* by Bruce Wilkinson. I was spellbound, as I could fully identify with his step-by-step explanation of the road to be traveled when the Lord provides a dream. The section on "Comfort Zone" issues truly hit home: "Your struggle with Comfort Zone issues reveals something important: You really do desire your Dream. Otherwise there would be no struggle. You're motivated to get into motion, but your desire to be comfortable stops you. So at this point in your life, comfort is the biggest enemy of your Dream.

"There's nothing the matter with wanting to be comfortable. But ultimately, Dreams are to help someone else. Comfort is to help yourself."[4]

From this extract, I understood not only to look to other people to fund my dream or vision while I remained in my own comfort zone. I instantly took the necessary steps and discussed with my family the need to fund specific areas of the Eduplex, only to realize later that the Lord was preparing me to step out of my comfort zone and into the gap once the donors withdrew. At the time, our family had no idea how the school would ever be able to afford repaying the interest-free loan.

Two and a half years later (September, 2009), we attended a conference in Zurich. A Swiss friend asked me whether I would be prepared to meet with an American acquaintance of his who wished to know more about my project and could be a possible donor. Although I was pressed for time, I agreed to meet with his friend on the Monday morning at nine.

Favor in God's Eyes

On the Saturday morning, Anita and I both prayed for the meeting. In her prayer, Anita said that we were inclined to ask for favor in the eyes of man, but that she would like to ask for favor in God's eyes. Her prayer remained with me during the entire weekend, as I thought about the meeting, how I had been ridiculed in the past because of my faith, and the vision the Lord had given me.

I repeatedly asked myself whether I should even mention the Lord's vision to this potential American donor, or simply call it "my vision". I realized that by omitting the fact that it was the Lord's vision, I might obtain favor in the eyes of man, but not in the eyes of the Lord. In fact, I would be denying Him. I decided to give a truthful account of what had happened and not let the possible loss of another donation influence my testimony.

Despite a severe bout of flu, I took a train to Zurich for my appointment on the Monday morning. My friend arranged a meeting room at his company and introduced me to the potential donor.

After we exchanged courteous greetings, he said, "Tell me about your project." I explained that the Lord gave me a vision in 1992 to make a difference in education for the deaf. Within a few minutes he asked, "What do you need?" I responded that we required partners to walk the road with us. Again, the question, "What do you need? Give it to me straight."

I replied that we had 75 deaf children in the school and that 35 of them received full bursaries, which resulted in a budget shortfall of approximately US$250,000 per year.

"Is that what you need?" he asked.

I started feeling very uncomfortable at that stage—discussing monetary needs rather than the vision—but he kept pressing me. I explained that our Swiss donors withdrew during the final phase of construction due to a church making use of our facilities on Sundays, and that our family had to borrow US$2 million to complete the Eduplex.

"Now your family has no money?" he asked.

I was unnerved by this man, a complete stranger, who kept on asking me all these direct questions.

"Yes," I replied.

And then the answer, "I will help you by covering 50% of the loan to your family by giving you €700,000" (approximately US$1,050,000).

I was completely stunned and lowered my head in my one hand. All I could say was, "Thank you Lord," before addressing him, "I don't know what to say; I am speechless."

He leaned forward, pointing his finger at me, and said, "I don't trust non-religious people and non-religious projects." At that moment, I realized that I would have lost a fortune had I denied the Lord that morning.

This remarkable meeting lasted 40 minutes and the money was transferred to our Foundation the very next day. After thanking him for his generosity, I received an SMS from him a few weeks later: "Sometimes a person finds oneself in a situation where he cannot save himself but he can save another. And in this situation, 'your faith hath saved you and your school'" (*verbatim*).

We truly serve an amazing God.

I learnt that when the Lord gives you a vision or a dream, it is imperative to spend time with Him in prayer and to meditate on His Word. You will need direction, encouragement and strength to fight fear and doubt, as well as the desire for your own comfort and financial security.

Author Os Hillman comments, "There is a time for everything. If God has called you to some endeavor and you are frustrated that it has not manifested, know that times of preparation and simmering are required before the vision can be achieved. Seldom does God call and manifest something at the same time. There is preparation. There is testing. There is relationship building between you and God that must take place. Once this is complete, you will see the vision materialize."[5]

Was it easy in my own life?

No.

During the first six years of getting Eduplex off the ground, we had endless challenges with management and staff—and it kept me on my knees. Very often, I was discouraged and even desperate, but the Lord, by His grace, sustained me as I sought His help and guidance. The adversities built character, so that in the end I could not take any credit for what had been achieved, but could only give Him all the honor and glory. During the time of preparation and the eventual execution of the vision, my relationship with the Lord continued to grow, as I saw one miracle after another taking place.

We are currently planning a second campus for the Eduplex, which will include a high school, a new Parent Guidance Centre, and a Training and Music Academy. Do we have the required US$20 million? No, but we have placed our faith in God to level the mountains before us, as He promised in Isaiah 45:1–3.

For more information on the Eduplex please view www.eduplex.co.za

CHAPTER 4

WHEN TROUBLE COMES

"How I plead with God, how I implore his mercy, pouring out my troubles before him. For I am overwhelmed and desperate, and you alone know which way I ought to turn to miss the traps my enemies have set for me. (There's one—just over there to the right!) No one gives me a passing thought. No one will help me; no one cares a bit what happens to me. Then I prayed to Jehovah. 'Lord,' I pled, 'you are my only place of refuge. Only you can keep me safe. Hear my cry, for I am very low. Rescue me from my persecutors, for they are too strong for me. Bring me out of prison, so that I can thank you. The godly will rejoice with me for all your help.'"

(Psalm 142:1–7)

Difficulties and Hardships

One thing we as businessmen can be sure of is that trouble will come. Despite performing our daily activities according to His will, we will still be confronted by challenges. In my experience, the enemy will *not* leave us alone while we try to follow the Lord and honor His name, especially when confessing that "Jesus is Lord" from a public platform. Trouble may often test our faith or character, and it is important to view our adversities as opportunities for growth and character-building.

We need to obey God and His principles and do what is right, irrespective of the challenges we face: "And let us not get tired of doing what is right, for after a while we will reap a harvest of blessing if we don't get discouraged and give up" (Galatians 6:9).

Over the years, I have come to realize that even God's loved ones still experience difficulties and hardships. The only way in which to counter the inevitable fear and panic flowing from adverse circumstances is to seek the Lord's face and to walk in faith, while clinging to the principles of obedience and integrity. In times of trouble and pressure we often seek to know what the future holds, but we should never try to exchange faith for knowledge. Enduring faith is far more precious than knowledge. By getting to know what the future holds, faith is no longer required.

The Bible's account of King Jehoshaphat's approach to difficult times (2 Chronicles 20) helped me a great deal in confronting the stress and panic often associated with business. A vast army was marching against Jehoshaphat from beyond the Dead Sea. Jehoshaphat was badly shaken by this news and determined to beg the Lord for help. He announced that all the people of Judah should fast in penitence and intercession before God.

Jehoshaphat publicly acknowledged his fear: "'We don't know what to do, but we are looking to you'" (2 Chronicles 20:12b). How often have I not found myself in a position where I simply did not know what to do.

As the people stood before the Lord, the Spirit of the Lord came upon one of the men and he proclaimed, "'The Lord says, 'Don't be afraid! Don't be paralyzed by this mighty army! For the battle is not yours, but God's! Tomorrow, go down and attack them! ... But you will not need to fight!

Take your places; stand quietly and see the incredible rescue operation God will perform for you, O people of Judah and Jerusalem! Don't be afraid or discouraged! Go out there tomorrow, for the Lord is with you!'" (2 Chronicles 20:15b–17).

The king and all the people of Judah and Jerusalem fell to the ground, worshipped the Lord and offered songs of praise that rang out strong and clear.

For those who aren't familiar with the rest of the account, Judah prepared for a battle with a difference. The choir was instructed to lead the march, praising and thanking the Lord. Along the way, King Jehoshaphat reminded the nation that God would provide them with victory: "'Believe in the Lord your God, and you shall have success!'" (2 Chronicles 20:20b). What a sight this must have been. A small group of people marching against the mighty armies with a choir upfront!

"And at the moment they began to sing and to praise, the Lord caused the armies of Ammon, Moab, and Mount Seir to begin fighting among themselves, and they destroyed each other!" (2 Chronicles 20:22). King Jehoshaphat and his people came away loaded with money, garments and jewels stripped from the corpses. They returned to Jerusalem full of joy that the Lord had rescued them from their enemies.

Jehoshaphat's Principles

On numerous occasions, Jehoshaphat's principles assisted me in solving what seemed to be insurmountable problems. Consider the timeless relevancy of Jehoshaphat's challenges—outlined in 2 Chronicles 20—from a contemporary perspective:

1. Challenge (verses 1–2): I have often faced major challenges in my life, some seemingly impossible to solve.
2. Panic (verse 3): I have often panicked before turning to God.
3. Prayer (verses 3–9): Seeking God's face, I shared my concerns and requested His help.

The view from our holiday home "Back to Basics" – a gift from God

The Ear Institute in Pretoria

The Eduplex Pre-school

The Eduplex Primary School

Former President Nelson Mandela and the author at the opening of the Eduplex, March 2002

"What you are doing here, is changing tragedy into triumph."
— Nelson Mandela

The open doors at the Eduplex depicting Revelation 3:8

The author and his wife Anita

4. Proposal (verses 15–17): When God revealed His will to me, I did my best to follow His instructions.
5. Praise (verses 18–19): I then thanked and praised Him for what He was about to do.
6. Preparation (verse 20): I prepared myself for "the battle" and did what I had to do. At times, I simply just had to trust the Lord. It is amazing how perceived problems often just seem to disappear. At other times, I had to re-examine the situation, prepare for "battle" and do my best, relying on God to provide victory. He has never disappointed me.
7. Focus (verse 20b): While going "into battle", I had to remind my family and staff that God would provide victory. Focusing the eyes of my staff on God has always been part of my responsibility as a Christian leader.
8. Peace (verse 30): Finally, when the problem was solved, the battle won and peace descended, we thanked God for His provision.

I read this Scripture for the first time just before the opening of our second Ear Institute, while members of the medical fraternity were organizing a boycott against our company and its products because of the chosen name. The ear, nose and throat (ENT) specialists felt the name "belonged" to them, even though they had neither registered, nor trade-marked the name and had never used it. The Dean of the Medical Faculty of a local university was due to deliver the opening address, but when the doctors threatened to boycott the university and the medical faculty, he had no option but to withdraw at the last minute.

I was disconcerted and then read Jehoshaphat's story. I sensed that the Lord wanted me to trust Him not only with regard to the opening, but also in the days, months and years ahead. In my experience, the Lord seldom gives an answer only for *the moment*. When He answers or gives a promise, it also relates to the future. I decided to perform the opening ceremony myself and to remind the guests that it was not I, but the Lord who had blessed and prospered our company.

That evening, I welcomed the 140 guests, some of whom had witnessed the miracles in our lives, and simply announced that the Dean was unable to attend due to unforeseen circumstances. No big deal and no mention of the drama that preceded the opening. In my address, I shared what the Lord had done for us over the years.

Amazing Grace

I asked a pastor friend to bless the Ear Institute and invited a Scottish piper to play "Amazing Grace", following the example of Jehoshaphat's choir leading the men into battle. I tried to follow the Lord's instructions exactly as He had given them to Jehoshaphat. Without exception, the guests commented that the ceremony was an event they would always remember. (Our offices are located in a residential neighborhood and I later heard that there was quite a stir over the piper "warming up" the pipes before his public presentation. We don't often hear Scottish pipers in our part of the world!)

The rest is history. This Ear Institute, by the Lord's grace and under the leadership of my wife Anita, is one of the most successful audiological practices in the country and a model for audiological services internationally. All the praise and honor must be given to God.

I am often still reminded of 2 Chronicles 20:17: "'But you will not need to fight! Take your places; stand quietly and see the incredible rescue operation God will perform for you, O people of Judah and Jerusalem! Don't be afraid or discouraged! Go out there tomorrow, for the Lord is with you!'"

Trying Times

Some challenges of being in business can of course be more trying than others. It is fair to say that businessmen often face a never-ending succession of problems, be it cash flow, competition, supply, foreign exchange, economic and political climate, credit, quality, staff, or even the weather. I have often wondered how businessmen who do not know the Lord, or those who do know the Lord but do not have a regular quiet time, manage their problems without experiencing major stress.

My quiet time consists of prayer, followed by reading from the Bible and three daily devotionals. It is remarkable how often the readings provide answers to my questions and decisions that need to be taken. For instance, the month of May always seems to bring with it a number of challenges. We have mainly elderly patients and during our winter (May to September), they prefer not to venture outdoors. Our business is normally slow during this time of the year and it plays havoc with our cash flow.

After praying about these problems, I read from C.H. Spurgeon's *Cheque Book of the Bank of Faith*. I believe that every day's message is intended for that specific day only, and therefore I never read in advance. However, on paging back, I came across a very encouraging "chronological" solution to the challenges we were experiencing.

- May 20, recommended reading: Isaiah 45:2: "I will go before you and will level the mountains; I will break down gates of bronze and cut through bars of iron" (NIV).

Spurgeon encourages the reader to go forward by faith and explains that the way will be cleared for us: "… the Lord himself will do the impossible for us, and the unexpected shall be a fact. Let us not sit down in coward fear. Let us press onward in the path of duty; for the Lord hath said it, 'I will go before you.' Ours (is) not to reason why; ours (is) but to dare and dash forward. It is the Lord's work, and he will enable us to do it …" [1]

- May 21, recommended reading: Ecclesiastes 11:3: "If clouds are full of water, they pour rain upon the earth" (NIV).

Spurgeon poses the question: "Why, then, do we dread the clouds which now darken our sky?" He continues, "True, for a while they hide the sun, but the sun is not quenched; he will shine out again before long. Meanwhile those black clouds are filled with rain; and the blacker they are, the more likely they are to yield plentiful showers. How can we have rain without clouds? Our troubles have always brought us blessings, and they always will … Our God may drench us with grief, but he will not drown us with wrath; nay, he will refresh us with mercy … O Lord, the clouds are the dust of thy feet! How near thou art in the cloudy and dark day! Faith sees the clouds emptying themselves and making the little hills rejoice on every side." [2]

- May 22, recommended reading: Psalm 138:7: "Though I am surrounded by troubles, you will bring me safely through them. You will clench your fist against my angry enemies! Your power will save me."

Spurgeon comments, "Wretched walking in the midst of trouble. Nay, blessed walking, since there is a special promise for it. Give me a promise, and what is the trouble?" He continues that when the Lord revives us, we shall have more life, more energy and more faith. "Is it not often so, that trouble revives us, like a breath of cold air when one is ready to faint?" he asks. "Pray to be revived thyself, and leave the rest with the Lord, who performeth all things for thee." [3]

Three wonderful answers to my prayers:

1. The Lord will go before me—I am not alone.
2. Fear not the unknown and the dark clouds, but continue your journey in faith.
3. The troubles might not disappear, but God will bring me safely through them and I will be revived.

Oftentimes, I receive the answers to my prayers in the Bible, which are then confirmed by my daily devotional readings; sometimes it is the other way round. And often I hear the still, tender voice of the Holy Spirit leading me to specific verses in His Word.

Bonus Time

In the midst of the worldwide financial crisis in 2008, we contemplated whether or not to pay our staff their annual bonuses due at the end of November. We had been in business since 1975 and had never failed to pay our staff their bonuses, which equates to one month's salary. But our turnover was down, and one department was down by as much as 50%!

Never had we been so divided about paying bonuses. Looking at the economic realities and not knowing what the future would hold, greatly influenced our decision-making. Were we entering a recession? Would we achieve our targets? Would we survive the credit crunch? I had already met with the new Principal of our school and agreed to pay the school staff their bonuses. We experienced a multitude of senior management problems prior to this appointment and the staff was not to blame for the fact that we could not find a suitable Principal. The only decision that remained was whether or not to pay our company staff their bonuses.

Eight days prior to the bonus pay-outs, I prayed about our predicament and our inability to reach consensus among us as a family. That morning, my devotional reading was from *Today God is First*. Author Os Hillman contends that during troubled and difficult times, we really discover how well we have been trained to withstand pressure and make the right decisions, regardless of outside influences: "… we fail under pressure usually because we reach a point where our ability to focus on execution yields to concern about outcome. This worry about outcome forces us to lose our concentration. The fear of failure begins to rule our emotions and actions, which ultimately results in our failure."

He uses the example of Jesus never yielding to pressure. None of His decisions were based on outcome; yet, He always made the right decision. The author concludes, "As God entrusts us with more and more responsibility, He brings more and more pressure into our lives to 'test the product', to make sure that He can give even more responsibility to us." [4]

The next day, I mentioned to Anita that I had to share an important lesson on bonuses with our son, Nico Junior. It was almost a prophetic utterance.

During my quiet time the next morning, I again prayed about the bonuses and the future of our company, and continued reading from *Today God is First*. Hillman relays the story of Joshua and Caleb who were led by the Spirit of God versus the spirit of fear. Caleb was a Romans 8:14 man!

"For if you live according to the sinful nature, you will die; but if by the Spirit you put to death the misdeeds of the body, you will live, because those who are led by the Spirit of God are sons of God" (Romans 8:13–14 NIV).

Caleb was led by the Spirit, not by fear. The author continues, "Fear prevents us from entering into what God has promised for each of us ... You cannot be led by fear, reason and analysis, or even skill. The Spirit must lead you." [5]

I instantly realized that, as head of our company, I had to make the decision whether or not to pay the bonuses. I could not delegate it to my son and other managers, as that would be putting unfair pressure on them. Their role was to decide *who* qualified for a bonus, and not *whether* we should be paying bonuses. I also realized that fear of the future would interfere with my decision—and if my decision stemmed from fear, I would not be acting according to the guidance of the Holy Spirit.

My second daily reading was from Max Lucado's *Grace for the Moment*, in which the author quotes 2 Timothy 2:13: "If we are not faithful, he will still be faithful, because he cannot be false to himself."

Lucado comments, "God's blessings are dispensed according to the riches of his grace, not according to the depth of our faith ... Why is that important to know? So you won't get cynical. Look around you. Aren't there more mouths than bread? Aren't there more wounds than physicians? Aren't there more who need the truth than those who tell it? So what do you do? Throw up your hands and walk away? Tell the world we can't help them? No, we don't give up. We look up. We trust. We believe. And our optimism is not hollow. Christ has proven worthy. He has shown that he never fails. That's what makes God, God." [6]

I was blown away! Of course, there were more mouths than bread! I pictured myself walking with a big loaf under my arm, breaking off pieces of bread and putting it into the open mouths of my staff. I realized yet again that it was my responsibility to see to the welfare of my staff, the people God entrusted to me. I simply could not throw up my hands and walk away, telling my staff I was unable to help! The Lord also reminded me of a saying that I often quote, "Don't give up; look up!" I knew I had to rely on the Lord to provide.

What made this experience even more remarkable is that I had a meeting scheduled at nine o'clock that same morning with a Christian brother who required my assistance to start a bakery. (One morning, at around one o'clock, God gave him an amazing formula for a fat-free, protein-rich bread baked with whey.) The Lord had promised success before we even started: there were indeed more mouths than bread!

I met with Nico Junior first thing that morning and shared with him what I believed the Lord wanted us to do. I explained that I had decided to pay bonuses to the staff and that he and his managers were to let me know who qualified and who didn't, due to their work not being up to standard. (I believe in the principle of good stewardship.) In fact, I said that from that day onwards we would operate in faith, by the grace of our Lord, always pay bonuses to those who qualified, and finally, that we would never have this discussion again.

My son enquired, "Dad, are you taking a bonus?" I said, "No, your mother and I will be giving our bonuses to the school in order for them to pay their staff bonuses." He replied, "I want you to do the same with mine."

I met with my friend, the baker, later that morning and agreed to assist him. Having searched for the right premises for quite some time, he opened his bakery in June 2009.

A Gift from God

That same afternoon, I had lunch with a friend. Upon my return to the office, I found our Chief Financial Officer waiting for me. She was clearly stressed and had tears in her eyes. In fact, I had never seen her in such a state. She explained that the bank had just phoned and that she had made a terrible mistake. The bank informed her that a forward exchange contract was due for payment and that we needed to pay the bank CHF1 million (approximately US$1 million).

She knew nothing about this contract though, and couldn't understand how she could have missed it. I was as much in the dark, as I managed all the contracts along with her. All our contracts were accounted for—and we definitely did not have such a contract.

She also told me that the bank informed her that we could postpone the contract, but that we would be much worse off in terms of the foreign exchange rate. We would lose thousands in the process and would immediately have to increase the cost of our products, most of which were imported. This was clearly not an option.

"What else did they say?" I prompted. She added that another option was to sell them the contract for CHF1.1 million (US$1.1 million).

"Pardon me?" I exclaimed.

Then only did she realize what the offer entailed. Due to the devaluation of our South African currency, the Rand, the contract was now worth more than the contract amount entered into and our profit would be CHF100,000 (US$100,000) without us having to pay one cent!

Was this a coincidence? No, this was a miracle. Yet again, God provided in a miraculous way. All He wished for us to do was to make the right decision with regard to the bonuses. He had already planned for our provision. We had no records of this forward exchange contract and our enquiries at the bank only led to one answer: "You entered into it; it is your responsibility."

The lesson in all of this was that without my regular quiet time, I would have acted out of fear and would not have paid the staff their bonuses, rather than having been led by the Holy Spirit.

Recognition

That same afternoon, I received a phone call from the Rector of the University of Pretoria informing me that the University Senate had decided to award me with the Chancellor's Medal for Outstanding Service to the Community, particularly for my work among the deaf. I phoned my friend Gerrit in the USA, and shared the day's experiences with him. His response was, "Hasn't the Lord got a wonderful sense of humor! Not only does He give you US$100,000, but also a medal as the cherry on top!"

Speaking to my son later, I said, "Nic, today the Lord taught us an amazing lesson. Do you think we can now take our bonuses, because this is no longer our own money, but a gift from God? Not only did He provide for our staff, but He also provided for us."

He smiled. "Yes Dad, I think we can." To God alone be the glory.

Perception and Reality

Winter came, and once again, our turnover was under pressure. We were in the midst of a credit crisis and thousands of miners were being laid off, which affected our hearing protection division. Panic set in. Following the example of Jehoshaphat, I prayed about the situation: "Lord," I said, "You know business is slow. You know that our suppliers are putting pressure on us for more sales. You know we are trying our best. Please show me whether there is something in my business or personal life that is not pleasing to You, so that I may rectify it. Lord, please show me what to do."

My readings that morning were from the following devotionals:

• *Cheque Book of the Bank of Faith* – C.H. Spurgeon

"For the LORD will not forsake his people for his great name's sake: because it hath pleased the LORD to make you his people" (1 Samuel 12:22).

Spurgeon comments, "By all the memories of the Lord's former loving-kindnesses let us rest assured that he will not forsake us … He has not wrought such wonders for us that he might leave us after all." [7]

• *Grace for the Moment* – Max Lucado

"I am the LORD, the God of every person on the earth. Nothing is impossible for me" (Jeremiah 32:27).

Lucado writes, "We need to hear that God is still in control. We need to hear that it's not over until he says so. We need to hear that life's mishaps and tragedies are not a reason to bail out. They are simply a reason to sit tight.

"Corrie ten Boom used to say, 'When the train goes through a tunnel and the world gets dark, do you jump out? Of course not. You sit still and trust the engineer to get you through.'" [8]

• *God Calling* – Edited by A.J. Russell

"Endeavour to put from you every thought of trouble. Take each day, and with no backward look, face the day's problem with Me, and seek My Help and guidance as to what you can do." [9]

• *Today God is First* – Os Hillman

"The lions may roar and growl, yet the teeth of the great lions are broken" (Job 4:10).

Hillman comments, "The enemy of our souls is very good at this game. He may bring on us what we perceive to be true when it is a lie. It may appear that there is no way around a situation. He may bring great fear on us. When we buy into this lie, we are believing only what we have chosen to perceive to be true. It usually has no basis of truth ... The next time some event comes into your life that creates fear and trembling, first determine the source. Look past the emotions and evaluate the situation in light of God's Word. Perception is not always reality." [10]

The Lord's response was perfectly clear:

1. He would not forsake me.
2. I needed to sit tight and trust Him through these difficult times, since nothing is impossible for Him.

3. I needed to check my own (negative) thoughts and face each day's challenges with Him.
4. I needed to be very careful of perceptions. I needed to get the facts, put aside the emotions and get to the truth.

What tremendous encouragement! I could face each day with confidence, not in myself, but in the Lord. He would keep on providing as He always did. Nothing is impossible for Him!

I trust that these experiences will encourage you to also *press into the Lord*, not only in difficult times, but also when times are good. He is worth pressing into and He will never forsake you, nor leave you. He promised, "You will find me when you seek me, if you look for me in earnest" (Jeremiah 29:13).

CHAPTER 5

FEAR

"Fight fear as you would fight a plague."

(Ed. A.J. Russell)

"He who you fear is only a man after all, while he who promises to comfort you is God, your Maker, and Creator of heaven and earth."

(C.H. Spurgeon)

Fertile Ground for Fear

Fear is probably one of the most debilitating emotions in the business world. It plays havoc with one's thoughts and one's actions, especially during the small hours of the night when things seem to be at their worst. I have often struggled with fear of failure, fear of poverty, and mainly, fear of people.

Trying to run a business in a developing country such as South Africa can be challenging at best. The world and its economic instabilities seem to be amplified in a country such as ours. Fluctuating exchange rates, unstable governments, an uncertain economic environment, high inflation levels, high interest rates (often between three to six times higher than in Europe and the USA), and poor planning and corruption invariably impact negatively on business strategies and expectations.

"High road" (success) and "low road" (failure) scenarios are bandied about, creating fertile ground for uncertainty and fear. "What if?" scenarios begin to plague one's thoughts, inevitably leading to a search for safe havens, fail-safe investments, guaranteed returns and hedging against currencies, only to realize that when a real crisis occurs, nothing is certain and everything becomes a risk.

We witnessed this in 1987, again in 2001 (after 9/11, when fear had a devastating effect on stock markets worldwide), and again in 2008–2010 during the credit crisis, when "solid" banks and financial institutions literally disappeared overnight. Billions were lost when raw fear and panic gripped people all over the world, resulting in stocks being sold and tens of thousands losing their jobs, homes and life-savings.

In his book, *The Call*, Rick Joyner writes about standing in a prison yard surrounded by massive walls. He observes people sitting in groups and others milling around, trying to find their own identity and a group most likely to accept them. On closer scrutiny, he sees deep wounds and multiple scars from old wounds.

He approaches some of the inmates and asks them why they are in prison. Without exception, they look at him in astonishment, declaring emphatically that they are not in prison. When he points at the fences and the guards, they reply, "What fences? What guards?" He then realizes that they are completely blinded by fear.

Joyner continues that one has to refrain from associating with people who are adamant to deprive you of your vision. "Discouragement," he says, "is usually the beginning of the loss of vision." [1]

What we need to realize is that "blindness" gradually sets in as we begin to notice and ponder everything happening around us. Being human, we tend to become discouraged, and fear slowly finds its way into our hearts.

Fear of Failure

You have not yet experienced true humiliation and fear until you've shaken hands with failure. What happens when you have tried everything in your power, only to be brought to a place where you realize that your own efforts have come to naught, and that bankruptcy is staring you in the face? An uncontrollable fear sets in. I've been there; I know how it feels.

It is a lonely place. In fact, thinking or planning even one day ahead becomes impossible. But, it is also a place where God can perform miracles if you will only trust Him. But to trust Him, you need to seek Him. As Jesus Himself said, "But seek first his kingdom and his righteousness, and all these things will be given to you as well. Therefore do not worry about tomorrow, for tomorrow will worry about itself. Each day has enough trouble of its own" (Matthew 6:33-34 NIV).

Os Hillman refers to these hardships as "desert experiences".

"What desert experience has He brought into your life lately?" he asks. "Whatever it is … do not fear the heat that is sure to come. He is walking beside you in order to test you and find out what is really in your heart. Ask for His grace to pass the test. He wants to bring all of His children into the Promised Land." [2]

After 9/11, the South African currency devalued dramatically against all major currencies. Every shipment was more expensive than the last, with prices increasing virtually every second week. Not only were our own imported products affected, but basic necessities like fuel and corn—the main staple food for the majority of South Africans—quadrupled in price.

As mentioned, our business caters mainly for the elderly. Experience has shown that whenever an economic crisis emerges, pensioners tend to clamp down, not wishing to spend money, particularly not on a "grudge purchase" such as hearing aids. This played havoc with our business.

As our turnover declined and our products became more expensive, our reserves started running out and we owed the bank millions. I found panic setting in as fear mounted. I distinctly remember asking the Lord for help and advice during my quiet times. What was I to do: borrow more money or simply close shop? I added that if it was His will for us to go into liquidation, He simply had to show me how to do it in a God-honoring way. God heard my cry for help.

My devotional reading one morning was from *Cheque Book of the Bank of Faith* and the recommended Bible reading Psalm 27:14: "Don't be impatient. Wait for the Lord, and he will come and save you! Be brave, stout-hearted and courageous. Yes, wait and he will help you."

Spurgeon continues that our waiting should be on the Lord and that He is worth waiting for. "He never disappoints the waiting soul. While waiting, keep up your spirits. Expect a great deliverance, and be ready to praise God for it." [3]

I was highly encouraged by Psalm 27:14 and the fact that the Lord answered my prayer in such an immediate, direct and positive way, showing me what to do in an impossible situation that was not of my own doing. Knowing that I had to do nothing but trust the Lord and continue with the work, while waiting on Him, provided immense relief.

However, there were three "heart tests" I first had to pass, before I would see any deliverance. These tests were not easy; in fact, they were battles!

Heart Test One: Liquidating our Stocks

After receiving the Scripture and commentary from Spurgeon, I continued to pray about our financial situation. I heard the Holy Spirit's gentle voice, "You can do something about it now." I asked, "What can I do Lord?" The Holy Spirit responded, "Put your own money into the company." I was shocked. Over the years, Anita and I had worked very hard to accumulate the little savings we had. Did the Lord expect me to plough all of this back into the company?

I panicked and thought, "Our money! What about our money?" and immediately 2 Chronicles 25:7–9 came to mind where Amaziah paid approximately US$200,000 to hire 100,000 experienced mercenaries from Israel. But a prophet arrived with a message from the Lord: "'Sir, do not hire troops from Israel, for the Lord is not with them. If you let them go with your troops to battle, you will be defeated no matter how well you fight; for God has power to help or to frustrate.'" Amaziah whined about the money and the prophet replied, "The Lord is able to give you much more than this!"

On realizing the significance of this passage, I immediately liquidated our stocks and paid whatever reserves we had into the company, knowing that the Lord would give us much more than that! Two months later, the second test came, with no relief in sight.

Heart Test Two: Paying Christmas Bonuses

After a very poor financial year, I realized that we could not afford to pay Christmas bonuses unless I took our hard-earned money, which we had paid into the company, and used that as bonuses for the staff. On the one hand, the very thought seemed like madness to me, but on the other, I knew the majority of our staff needed the bonus more than ever due to the drastic increases in transport and food.

Corn, like fuel, is linked to the international price in US$. A devaluing currency has an immediate impact on the price of corn and transport due to the increased fuel price. The average South African household spends up to a third, and in some cases even more, of their income on transport costs. Add to that a quadrupling in the price of their staple food, corn (polenta), and low-salaried citizens really battle to make ends meet.

During that time, Isaiah 58 provided the answers to my predicament: "'We have fasted before you,' they say. 'Why aren't you impressed? Why don't you see our sacrifices? Why don't you hear our prayers? We have done much penance, and you don't even notice it!' I'll tell you why! Because you are living in evil pleasure even while you are fasting, and you keep right on oppressing your workers … No, the kind of fast I want is that you stop oppressing those who work for you and treat them fairly and give them what they earn … Feed the hungry! Help those in trouble!" (Isaiah 58:3, 6, 10).

And then the promise in verses 11–12: "And the Lord will guide you continually, and satisfy you with all good things, and keep you healthy too; and you will be like a well-watered garden, like an ever-flowing spring. Your sons will rebuild the long-deserted ruins of your cities …"

I acknowledged that I was responsible for looking after my staff—the very people the Lord entrusted to me—and to care for their general wellbeing and prosperity. In turn, the Lord would care for my wellbeing, and that of my children and their children. What an amazing promise.

Needless to say, it remained a tough decision to pay our staff their bonuses. Isaiah 58 was clear on this issue, but I had to overcome my own fears first. Once the decision was made, I had complete peace. Did our turnover increase from one month to the next? No, it did not. We were still in difficult financial times, but the exchange rate started to improve[*], which resulted in our imported goods becoming cheaper. But, there was yet more to come.

Heart Test Three: Giving Increases

Before and after Christmas, business remained quiet. We entered the new year wondering what the future would bring, as we barely made it from one month to the next. Staff salaries are normally revised annually at the beginning of March, the start of our new financial year.

---

[*] Our currency, the Rand, appreciated so much against all major currencies that the government appointed a Commission of Enquiry to investigate the cause of the major currency fluctuation. No cause was found and neither the collapse, nor improvement could be explained. Could this have been a miraculous intervention by the Lord?

Given the previous year's poor financial performance and our debt to the bank, increasing our staff's salaries just did not make any economic sense. After all, they did receive their Christmas bonuses …

How could we now provide increases with money we did not have? I ignored Isaiah 58 (done that Lord; and moved on!) and while praying about the increases, I experienced a real leanness in my spirit. Not a word from the Lord. I searched, asked and begged, "Lord, what should I do?" Not a word—nothing.

I then thought of bargaining with the Lord. If I gave 2%, surely that was better than nothing? Still, no response. "But, Lord," I insisted, "perhaps 4%, or maximum 5%!" I was aware that inflation was running way beyond the percentages I had contemplated. Still, no word from God. Desperation set in.

One morning, whilst shaving, I thought about this strange phenomenon. I asked the Lord and had no response to all my prayers. Why? I suddenly heard the Holy Spirit ask me in a clear voice, "What increase would you like?" I was stunned. I immediately knew the answer to my prayers.

John 8 came to mind. Jesus often responds to our prayers in an indirect way. The Jewish leaders and Pharisees brought to Jesus a woman caught in the act of adultery.

"'Teacher,' they said to Jesus, 'this woman was caught in the very act of adultery. Moses' law says to kill her. What about it?' They were trying to trap him into saying something they could use against him, but Jesus stooped down and wrote in the dust with his finger. They kept demanding an answer, so he stood up again and said, 'All right, hurl the stones at her until she dies. But only he who never sinned may throw the first!'" The accusers all slipped away.

"Then Jesus stood up again and said to her, 'Where are your accusers? Didn't even one of them condemn you?' 'No sir,' she said. And Jesus said, 'Neither do I. Go and sin no more'" (John 8:4–11).

"Lord, what percentage increase should I give?"

"What increase would *you* like, my son?"

Checkmate! I was hoping for 10%!

Notwithstanding, I still tried to reason my way out of the 10%. As the Chief Executive Officer, I could give my staff members a 5% increase and pay myself a bonus, but I soon realized that this was not what God expected from me. He expected total obedience to the answer He gave me: to pay my staff exactly the same bonus as the percentage I envisaged for myself—nothing more, nothing less. That morning, I shared my experience with my management team. 10% was what I wanted, and 10% was what we were to pay our staff.

The tests became more difficult, as I had moved some of our own money by faith to pay the staff their bonuses and a salary increase. Three tough heart tests, but by God's grace, I managed to obey. It was not easy, but it was a "desert experience" never to be forgotten.

Ten days after deciding to give the 10% increase, I had a meeting with our bank to discuss the renewal and possible increase of our overdraft facilities. Our banker asked me, "What happened?"

It transpired that we did not need an increase in our facilities. Instead of us owing the bank, the bank now owed us money! Millions literally flowed into our bank accounts from the moment the third heart test was passed. We were baffled; we tried to explain it as a possible knock-on effect of the improved exchange rate, as well as our debtors releasing funds owed to us over a lengthy period. Yet, for me, this was a miracle. I expected a great deliverance, and when it came, I praised God for it. Relief came, but I had to pass the tests first.

I learnt a very valuable lesson: You can trust God to deliver in difficult times, provided you are *obedient* to His guidance and instructions.

Over the past eight years, our company statements reflected a 600% increase in turnover. And the money? What about the money? The Lord gave us much more than what we had to forfeit to help our staff!

Fear of Man

In 1998, our executive team prayed and asked God for a new company strategy. We believed that God showed us to open Ear Institutes, professional audiological facilities, to offer a world-class professional service and equipment for the hearing impaired. I have never believed God to be satisfied with second best. As Christians, we have to offer our patients the very best service at the best price, thereby honoring the Lord.

As mentioned previously, we opened our first Ear Institute and the second one soon followed. The ENT specialists then started taking notice and claimed that the words "Ear Institute" belonged to them and them alone. I disagreed, as an "Institute" is a society or organization for the promotion of science, education, etc. (according to *The Concise Oxford Dictionary*, 9th edition). We did research, trained students and professionals, and attended to patients.

The ENT doctors declared "war" on our organization and we were insulted and called all sorts of names. Slanderous articles appeared in their Society's news bulletin and complaints were lodged with the Health Professions Council of South Africa, as well as with our main suppliers, urging them to refrain from supplying us.

During that time, Nehemiah's struggle to rebuild the walls of Jerusalem and the resistance he encountered meant a lot to me. When he started rebuilding the wall, Sanballat, Tobiah and Geshem the Arab heard of the plan. They scoffed and said, "'What are you doing, rebelling against the king like this?' But I replied, 'The God of heaven will help us, and we, his servants, will rebuild this wall; but you may have no part in this affair'" (Nehemiah 2:19–20).

Sanballat was very angry. He insulted and mocked Nehemia and his workers, and laughed at them (Nehemiah 4:1). Finally, Sanballat, Tobiah and Geshem sent a message to Nehemiah, enquiring whether they could work together. Nehemiah realized that they were intent on sabotaging his efforts. But he sought his refuge in the Lord, praying for strength, whilst encouraging his workers.

Something similar happened with the ENTs. After the name-calling, the insults and the complaints, I was invited to a meeting to discuss whether we could resolve the issue and work together. I traveled to Cape Town to meet with members of a Regional Committee. Their stance was that if we were prepared to change our name, we would enjoy their full support. I immediately knew that this was a trap, but I agreed to consider it and to inform them of my decision in due course.

We spent our December vacation at our holiday home in Vermont. I often use this time of leisure to pray, think and plan for the year ahead. I specifically recall praying about the request of the ENTs, simply because I did not want to cling to a name because of my own pride or ego. I placed the name at the Lord's feet and prayed about it every morning, asking for His guidance.

There was tremendous pressure on me to change the name, and finally, the answer came from Isaiah 51:12–16 during my quiet time: "I, even I, am he who comforts you and gives you all this joy. So what right have you to fear mere mortal men, who wither like the grass and disappear? And yet you have no fear of God, your Maker—you have forgotten him, the one who spread the stars throughout the skies and made the earth. Will you be in constant dread of men's oppression, and fear their anger all day long?

"For I am the Lord your God, the Lord Almighty, who dried a path for you right through the sea, between the roaring waves. And I have put my words in your mouth and hidden you safe within my hand. I planted the stars in place and molded all the earth. I am the one who says to Israel, 'You are mine.'"

Jeremiah 17:5–7 accentuated this truth: "The Lord says: Cursed is the man who puts his trust in mortal man and turns his heart away from God … But blessed is the man who trusts in the Lord and has made the Lord his hope and confidence."

Another valuable lesson: Our Lord provides and we should rely on Him and not on the empty promises of doctors and specialists. We prayerfully decided on the name "Ear Institute" in the first place and we would dishonor God by letting our fear of man get the better of us.

God's Word emphasizes the consequences of a doubtful mind: "If you want to know what God wants you to do, ask him, and he will gladly tell you, for he is always ready to give a bountiful supply of wisdom to all who ask him; he will not resent it. But when you ask him, be sure that you really expect him to tell you, for a doubtful mind will be as unsettled as a wave of the sea that is driven and tossed by the wind; and every decision you then make will be uncertain, as you turn first this way, and then that. If you don't ask with faith, don't expect the Lord to give you any solid answer" (James 1:5–8).

I asked God, He guided me, and I decided to keep the name. To date, we have 17 Ear Institutes throughout Southern Africa.

What happened to the doctors and other professionals who complained? During this time of oppression, the Lord provided the following promise in Isaiah 51:22b–23: "'See, I take from your hands the terrible cup; you shall drink no more of my fury; it is gone at last. But I will put that terrible cup into the hands of those who tormented you and trampled your souls to the dust and walked upon your backs.'"

I never retaliated. I turned my focus to that which God had given me to do in the first place, and God took care of the rest.

Overcoming Fear

I learnt an important lesson. As a Christian, one is often faced with two choices in difficult situations: Choosing the road of fear by being disobedient and depending on your own wisdom and understanding, or choosing the road of faith by being obedient and trusting wholly in the Lord, no matter how difficult it may be. The one leads to enslavement or even death, the other to a wonderful promise of a preserved and safe life.

Jeremiah's warning to King Zedekiah is a sobering account of one man's choice to walk the road of fear, rather than to obey God: "'The Almighty Lord, the God of Israel, says: If you will surrender to Babylon, you and your family shall live and the city will not be burned. If you refuse to surrender, this city shall be set afire by the Babylonian army and you will not escape'" (Jeremiah 38:17–18).

Despite this warning, Zedekiah was afraid to surrender. But the Babylonians caught him as he fled the city in fear and made him watch as they killed his children and all the nobles of Judah. Then they gouged out his eyes and bound him in chains to send him away to Babylon as a slave (Jeremiah 39:5–7). Had Zedekiah not been afraid, he and his family would have lived. His disobedience because of fear cost him dearly.

This stands in stark contrast to the word given to Ebed-melech, the Ethiopian, in Jeremiah 39:18: "As a reward for trusting me, I will preserve your life and keep you safe."

In *God Calling*, the two listeners relay God's response to fear: "Love and fear cannot dwell together. By their very natures they cannot exist side by side. Evil is powerful, and fear is one of evil's most potent forces ... You can only banish fear by My Presence and My Name." [4]

On a Personal Note

Soon after the heart tests, I felt led to discuss with our bank the release of all personal sureties held by them in favor of our company.

The bankers laughed and said that it would not be possible. We had to carry some risk for the company and our request was totally unreasonable. I persisted and asked them to rather look at what credit facilities could be offered to the company, without us having to sign any surety. Should this be granted, we would just have to make ends meet.

I took Proverbs 6:1–5 as a guide, even if we were to sign surety for our own company: "Son, if you endorse a note for someone you hardly know, guaranteeing his debt, you are in serious trouble. You may have trapped yourself by your agreement. Quick! Get out of it if you possibly can! Swallow your pride; don't let embarrassment stand in the way. Go and beg to have your name erased. Don't put it off. Do it now. Don't rest until you do. If you can get out of this trap you have saved yourself like a deer that escapes from a hunter, or a bird from the net."

Within weeks the bank informed us that due to the company's history with the bank, which reflected sound performance and profitability, we were released from all our sureties with immediate effect and without a change to our existing lines of credit. The different companies had to sign surety for each other, which was fully understandable and fair.

Proverbs 22:1 (NIV) and Isaiah 55:5b came to mind: "A good name is more desirable than great riches; to be esteemed is better than silver or gold." And "... not because of your own power or virtue but because I, the Lord your God, have glorified you."

CHAPTER 6

INTEGRITY

"My son, listen to me and do as I say,
and you will have a long, good life.
I would have you learn this great fact:
that a life of doing right is the wisest life there is.
If you live that kind of life, you'll not limp or
stumble as you run.
Carry out my instructions; don't forget them, for
they will lead you to real living.
Don't do as the wicked do.
Avoid their haunts—turn away, go somewhere
else, for evil men can't sleep until they've done
their evil deed for the day."

(Proverbs 4:10–16)

Ethical Decline

The current business environment seems to be characterized by an epidemic of ethical decline. Many top executives are guilty of manipulating balance sheets and overstating profits and assets in their quest to enrich themselves, while investors (many of them pensioners) lose millions as companies go into liquidation, or their stock prices collapse.

Pastor R. Kent Hughes, author of *Disciplines of a Godly Man*, says the following: "The colossal slide of integrity (especially masculine ethics) has grim spiritual, domestic, and political implications which threaten the survival of life as we know it. But for the Christian, the most chilling fact is this: there is little statistical difference between the ethical practices of the religious and the nonreligious."

Hughes ascribes this integrity crisis to the fact that humans are "fundamentally dishonest" and "congenital liars". He continues, "No one had to instruct us in the art of dishonesty. Even once we are regenerated, if we do not discipline ourselves under the Lordship of Christ, we return to deceit like a duck to water." [1]

Harsh words, yes, but you and I know it to be the truth. The Bible cites numerous examples of people with no or little integrity. In 1 Samuel 15, Saul is instructed to destroy the nation of Amelek, but he keeps part of the spoils, including the choicest cattle. When confronted by the prophet Samuel, he responds that the spoils are to be sacrificed to God, thus condoning his wrongful actions.

Samuel replies, "'Has the Lord as much pleasure in your burnt offerings and sacrifices as in your obedience? Obedience is far better than sacrifice. He is much more interested in your listening to him than in your offering the fat of rams to him'" (1 Samuel 15:22).

In my own walk as a Christian businessman, I have made many mistakes, often driven by self-interest, greed, lust, materialism and pride.

Integrity – Knowing the Difference between Right and Wrong

The apostle Paul highlights the importance of integrity: " ... for I want you always to see clearly the difference between right and wrong, and to be inwardly clean, no one being able to criticize you from now until our Lord returns" (Philippians 1:10).

Soon after accepting Christ into my life, I attended church one morning and the pastor announced that the sermon would revolve around the topic of money. I recall sitting back thinking that there was not much to learn. As I listened to him, I suddenly became aware of a warm sensation on the top of my head. I looked around, thinking it might be the sun shining through a window, but it turned out not to be. Then I heard a voice saying, "Why don't you trust me with your money?"

I was taken aback, hoping that nobody would see the strong beam of light shining on my head. I knew intuitively that this was the Lord speaking to me and that He was referring to my "little drawer" containing my "hot money", which I had never declared to the tax authorities.

"Lord, you know I can't afford to pay my tax, as I won't have enough money to live on or provide for my family," was my silent response.

He replied, "Trust Me!"

The warm sensation disappeared immediately. I was in shock. This was the last thing I expected to experience that morning. As Anita and I left the church, I shared this encounter with her. "We can never go back to our old ways," I said, "We will have to trust the Lord to provide." The next morning, I banked every cent in my "little drawer" and felt a tremendous relief, as I knew I was doing the right thing.

Since then, I have not had a day's worry about paying tax, or where the money would come from to pay any tax that may be due to the Revenue Services. I can testify to the fact that over the years our turnover increased whenever our taxes became due, and then returned to normal again. There has been no cyclical explanation and this has been the pattern for more than 30 years. Whenever our taxes become due, we experience God's provision in supernatural ways.

God's Word underscores the principle of obedience: "Obey the government, for God is the one who has put it there. There is no government anywhere that God has not placed in power ... Pay your taxes too ... pay your taxes and import duties gladly ..." (Romans 13:1–7).

A Good Deal versus A Fair Deal

I love it when a plan comes together; don't we all?

Part of our company's strategy is to expand our Ear Institutes, not only to enlarge our footprint in our country, but also to protect our market share. Some agents have sold their practices to us as they retired, or decided to rather join us and become part of a larger company with the stability it offers in terms of medical insurance, pension fund and life cover equal to four times their annual salary.

One of our agents, whom I have known since he was a student, always wanted to become a farmer. After establishing a very successful hearing-aid business, he decided to sell to us. We discussed the price and I explained to him that once he left, the turnover would inevitably drop as a new manager took over. In view of this, we could not pay him his asking price. The amount I offered was substantially less.

With some persuasion, we agreed on the price and also that he was to continue for approximately eight months, after which we would officially take over and pay him the agreed amount.

To my surprise, the business virtually doubled in turnover from the date of our agreement. Close to the takeover date, he asked to continue for another six months, as the business was doing so well. We agreed and the business continued to grow.

When I eventually handed him the check for the originally agreed selling price, I asked whether he was happy. He hesitated for a moment and then replied, "Yes." The business continued to perform exceptionally well and each time people asked how things were going, I gloated about the fantastic acquisition. And then, one morning during my quiet time, I read from Spurgeon's *Cheque Book of the Bank of Faith*. The recommended Bible reading was Proverbs 28:13: "A man who refuses to admit his mistakes can never be successful. But if he confesses and forsakes them, he gets another chance."

Spurgeon explains that a guilty and repenting sinner should " … cease from the habit of covering sin. This is attempted by falsehood, which denies sin; by hypocrisy, which conceals it; by boasting, which justifies it; and by loud profession, which tries to make amends for it … The sinner's business is to confess and forsake."

He continues, "We must not throw the fault upon others, nor blame circumstances, nor plead natural weakness. We must make a clean breast of it, and plead guilty to the indictment. There can be no mercy till this is done." [2]

I realized that the Lord was not happy with my transaction. The one verse which kept mulling through my mind as I boasted about "my bargain" was Proverbs 20:14: "'Utterly worthless!' says the buyer as he haggles over the price. But afterwards he brags about his bargain!"

I knew my integrity and the Lord's honor were at stake—and that I had to rectify the situation. The "good deal" was to become a "fair deal". I also realized that I could not expect the Lord's blessing on our endeavors if all concerned were not treated fairly.

40% more than the agreed price came to mind. I heard Satan whisper, "Surely, a deal is a deal? This is madness, people will think you have lost it! Nobody has ever gone back and paid more for a company after the deal had been signed and sealed! This is not what good business is about!" I knew that if I did not act there and then, Satan's reasoning would get the better of me.

I immediately phoned the agent and asked him to come and see me. He arrived a few days later and I explained what the Lord had revealed to me. I apologized. At first, he looked down, then looked me straight in the eye and said, "Nico, my wife and I knew that you paid us too little, but we decided to leave it to the Lord."

At that very moment, I saw my own sinful heart. I knew that this man was on a spiritual level I would never attain. Here was a man who trusted the Lord completely! Had I been in his shoes, I would never have sold my business for less than it was worth. I was greedy, and simply did not have the faith or the moral fiber to "leave it to the Lord". A humbling lesson, never to be forgotten—and a better understanding of Proverbs 16:11: "The Lord demands fairness in every business deal. He established this principle."

Some years later, I was reminded of this incident and also had to pay a lady 50% more than the amount originally agreed upon, as I remembered that the Lord demands fairness in every business deal: "He that walketh uprightly, walketh surely" (Proverbs 10:9).

Walking uprightly, with integrity, should be our aim. Although it might not bring wealth, it will certainly bring peace. Jesus said, "What profit is there if you gain the whole world—and lose eternal life?" (Matthew 16:26).

Os Hillman reminds Christian business people to ensure that their practices are righteous in God's sight. "If not," he says, "we can expect the enemy to be released to judge that sin. Ask the Lord today if there is any unrighteousness in your business practices that makes you vulnerable to judgment." [3]

"Whenever we act without God's blessing on our activity, we can expect God to thwart our plans," Hillman warns. He poses the question whether the Lord is able to bless our enterprises today. "If not, you may need to go back and clean up a few things before He can do so. Take whatever steps are needed to ensure the blessing of God today." [4]

I was forced to re-assess my own business practices in light of God's Word: "Don't copy the behavior and customs of this world, but be a new and different person with a fresh newness in all you do and think. Then you will learn from your own experience how his ways will really satisfy you" (Romans 12:2).

I also had to re-evaluate my own attitude towards the government and taxes in light of Paul's letter to the Romans: "Obey the government, for God is the one who has put it there. There is no government anywhere that God has not placed in power. So those who refuse to obey the laws of the land are refusing to obey God, and punishment will follow ... Obey the laws, then, for two reasons: first, to keep from being punished, and second, just because you know you should ... Pay your taxes too, for these same two reasons ... Pay everyone whatever he ought to have: pay your taxes and import duties gladly, obey those over you, and give honor and respect to all those to whom it is due" (Romans 13:1–2, 5–8, 13b–14).

Paul's instructions are clear: Be a responsible citizen and a responsible Christian in all your dealings and do not bend the rules to suit your own agenda.

Integrity and Situational Ethics

Os Hillman contends, "Truth never changes. It is absolute. When we make decisions based on other actions that are taken, we move into making decisions based on the situation, not truth and righteousness."

He cites the example of an executive who resigned from a company. According to her work agreement, she was entitled to a bonus which management refused to pay. She simply decided to keep the company's laptop in exchange for the bonus she never received. However, she felt increasingly uneasy about this decision and concluded that the Holy Spirit was telling her to confess her wrongdoing. She called her former employer and explained what she had done. He accepted her apology, forgave her—and allowed her to keep the laptop.

"Have you had any experiences in which you have used situational ethics?" Hillman asks. He concludes, "The Lord desires His people to have a higher standard, even at the cost of being wronged. Ask the Lord to reveal any business practices that may indicate situational ethics. You might be surprised what will happen when you do the right thing." [5]

This extract reminded me of an incident in my childhood. Years ago, we used to celebrate Guy Fox Day in our country with fireworks—an old English tradition to commemorate the attempt by Mr. Fox to blow up the Houses of Parliament in London. I went to the local department store and bought a small bag of assorted fireworks. Once home, I realized that the lady at the store charged me much less than the price stated on the packet. I discussed it with my father and he suggested I go back, ask for the manager and pay him the extra money, which I did.

On the "big day", our doorbell rang and someone asked for me. Mr. Cohen, the manager of the store, personally came to thank me for my honesty and brought me a fantastic box full of fireworks as a "thank you" gift. As a young boy, my first brush with honesty was a very positive experience.

I have a habit of always checking my restaurant bills. It is amazing to see how often some items are not charged for. In exceptional cases, I am overcharged. Once, while holidaying in the Cape, I took my family out to lunch. On checking the bill, I noticed there was no charge for two salads we had ordered. I brought it to the attention of the manager and she replied, "Consider it a gift." That afternoon, I bought six bread rolls, only to find seven in the packet. Once again, I brought this to the attention of the manager and she said, "This must be your lucky day!"

It's Not About Me!

Whilst studying in Potchefstroom, Anita and I used to travel to Pretoria every weekend to visit her mother. Our vehicle was an old Opel Record, her mother's wedding gift to us.

As a young man, I drove quite fast and wanted to replace the headlights with halogen globes so that I could see better at night and drive even faster. One Saturday, I called on a small garage called Signorelli Motors in Pretoria and bought two halogen globes. In paying, I realized I was about US$2 short. I asked the owner whether I could pay him the following Monday.

His words upset me: "You students, you are all the same, you promise to pay and then you never do." I remember pointing my finger at my chest, saying, "I *will* come and pay you—I am not a thief."

That Monday came and went and every time I drove past the garage, I was reminded of my debt.

30 years later, I attended a weekend city conference hosted by a local congregation. An 80-year old gentleman stood up to give his testimony. As a young man, he bought a bicycle on credit from an Indian trader. Every month he paid his debt, but when he was transferred to another town he stopped paying.

After accepting Christ into his life, he was convicted by the Holy Spirit to go back to this trader and to pay his debt in full. He explained the reason for his visit to the Indian shopkeeper. The man responded that he was the first thief to come back and pay his debt. Then this gentleman said something that struck a nerve: "I realized that by paying my debt, it was not about me, but about the honor of God. I am sure that one day, I am going to meet this shopkeeper in heaven."

I immediately thought of my own US$2 outstanding debt and felt ashamed. The next day I calculated how much the amount would be with compound interest and started writing out the check. I like round figures and as I was about to round the amount off, I heard the Holy Spirit's soft voice, "Leave it as is." Again, I attempted to round the amount off and again the instruction, "Leave it as is." I wrote the correct amount on the check, including the cents.

The following Monday I phoned Signorelli Motors and asked to speak to Mr. Signorelli. "Junior or Senior?" the receptionist asked. I asked to speak to the father. I made an appointment to see him that afternoon without mentioning the reason for my visit. I wrote a letter explaining that the Holy Spirit persuaded me to repay my outstanding debt with interest, and asked for his forgiveness. I concluded the letter by expressing the hope that his son was as big a blessing to his business as my sons were to mine.

I arrived at the garage and noticed that the years had been good to the Signorellis and that they also had a successful business. I asked to see Mr. Signorelli Senior, but as I started to speak, my emotions got the better of me. I handed him the envelope with my letter and the check, and left.

A few days later, I received a phone call from Mr. Signorelli Junior. I immediately assumed that they were unhappy and that I was about to be reprimanded. On answering the phone, I apologized again, and then Mr. Signorelli Junior said the following: "Mr. Van der Merwe, there is no need to apologize. Let me tell you a story. My mother and I know the Lord. My father is getting to know the Lord. I don't know how you calculated the amount you gave us, but I find it very interesting that my father and I discussed writing off a long outstanding debt. That discussion took place over the weekend and we eventually decided to write it off, only to find that the very next day you walked in and gave my father a check for the exact amount we decided to write off."

I went cold as I realized that it was not about me; it is always about the honor of God. Like the 80-year old gentleman, I can also say that I am looking forward to meeting Mr. Signorelli Senior in heaven one day.

In his book, *Grace for the Moment*, Max Lucado addresses the issue of integrity: "I have something against the lying voices that noise our world. You've heard them. They tell you to swop your integrity for a new sale. To barter your convictions for an easy deal. To exchange your devotion for a quick thrill. They whisper. They woo. They taunt. They tantalize. They flirt. They flatter … The world rams at your door; Jesus taps at your door. The voices scream for your allegiance; Jesus softly and tenderly requests it. The world promises flashy pleasure; Jesus promises a quiet dinner … with God. Which voice do you hear?" [6]

CHAPTER 7

LUST, MATERIALISM AND PRIDE

"Above all else, guard your affections.
For they influence everything else in
your life."

(Proverbs 4:23)

"I warned the proud to cease their arrogance! I
told the wicked to lower their insolent gaze, and
to stop being stubborn and proud. For promotion
and power come from nowhere on earth,
but only from God.
He promotes one and deposes another."

(Psalm 75:4–7)

"For wisdom hates pride, arrogance, corruption
and deceit of every kind."

(Proverbs 8:13b)

Lust, materialism and pride … the downfall of so many of us.

Over the years, I have come to realize that I just cannot trust myself or rely on my own insights. My thoughts, judgments and actions are flawed, unless I seek the Lord's presence, the wisdom of His Word and the advice of trusted Christian friends.

King Solomon did not ask God for riches, but for wisdom and insight. In Proverbs, he says, "If you want favor with both God and man, and a reputation for good judgment and common sense, then trust the Lord completely; don't ever trust yourself. In everything you do, put God first, and he will direct you and crown your efforts with success" (Proverbs 3:5–6). He adds, "Getting wisdom is the most important thing you can do! And with your wisdom, develop common sense and good judgment" (Proverbs 4:7).

We covet that which we cannot have, we collect that which we do not really need, and then, once we have it all, we forget the Lord our God who gave it to us in the first place. This opens the door for sin.

Lust

In her book, *The Snare*, Lois Mowday Rabey takes a frank look at sexual immorality. "Most people don't plan to have an affair," she says, "And most of them think it could never happen to them. Because they don't recognize the subtle danger signs, they can suddenly find themselves in a dangerous relationship—with devastating consequences.

"It can start off innocently enough. Someone cares enough to pay attention. To look into your eyes. To touch with understanding. Even with the best motives, it's easy to slip gradually, almost imperceptibly, into the snare of an emotional or sexual entanglement." [1]

King David also fell victim to an adulterous affair. One night he couldn't get to sleep and went for a stroll on the roof of the palace. As he looked out over the city, he noticed a beautiful woman taking her evening bath (2 Samuel 11).

Is this not enough to get the blood racing in any male? How many of us have the will and inclination to turn away from temptation? A friend of mine succumbed to the relentless world of Internet pornography. I admired him for his courage to publicly admit that he had a problem and to ask for prayer. It took him years to free himself of this addiction and it nearly cost him his family. I remember how upset he was when he found out his wife had an affair, despite him having had numerous affairs in cyber space.

When Jesus teaches about lust in the Gospels, He says, "The laws of Moses said: 'You shall not commit adultery.' But I say: Anyone who even looks at a woman with lust in his eye has already committed adultery with her in his heart" (Matthew 5:27–28).

Proverbs 4:23–27 cautions, "Above all else, guard your affections. For they influence everything else in your life. Spurn the careless kiss of a prostitute. Stay far from her. Look straight ahead; don't even turn your head to look. Watch your step. Stick to the path and be safe. Don't sidetrack; pull back your foot from danger."

Pornography is a snare with devastating consequences—not only for men, but for women too. If you have a problem with pornography, take action! Find someone to lock your laptop or PC with a password unknown to you. Ask the hotel reception to disable the "pay-per-view" movies on your hotel television, or better still, only stay in hotels that do not have "pay-per-view" channels. (Unfortunately, these are often the more expensive hotels.) Remember Proverbs 6:32–33: "But the man who commits adultery is an utter fool, for he destroys his own soul. Wounds and constant disgrace are his lot …"

Lois Mowday Rabey writes that one of the causes of immorality is being vulnerable. Vulnerability implies added risk. People are vulnerable because they have been wounded or are weary; because they are emotionally run down, their defenses are down and everything is seen through an emotional filter.

She adds that one of the most common forms of stress that leads to broken relationships is that of burnout. "When a person is exhausted, he is in a very vulnerable position. He simply cannot think as clearly as someone who is healthy." [2]

Extended periods away from one's spouse can also lead to tempting situations, which could be avoided if we limit our time away from home. Take responsibility, slow down, be accountable to trusted friends and maintain the basics: stay in the Word, have regular quiet times, pray often and seek fellowship with fellow believers.

Author of *Battling Unbelief*, John Piper, writes, "So I have learned again and again from firsthand experience that there are many professing Christians who have a view of salvation that disconnects it from real life, and that nullifies the threats of the Bible, and puts the sinning person who claims to be a Christian beyond the reach of biblical warnings. I believe this view of the Christian life is comforting thousands who are on the broad way that leads to destruction (Matthew 7:13)." He continues, "Jesus said, if you don't fight lust, you won't go to heaven. Not that saints always succeed. The issue is that we resolve to fight, not that we succeed flawlessly." [3]

Piper refers to the apostle Peter who warned, "Abstain from the passions of the flesh, which wage war against your soul" (1 Peter 2:11), and the apostle Paul who listed immorality, impurity, and sensuality as sins that would prevent us from inheriting the kingdom of God (Galatians 5:19–21).

Anita and I have been married for nearly 40 years. I proposed after only one month of getting to know her. We got engaged six months later and tied the knot 14 months after our first meeting. She is four years my senior—and fortunately, "one of us had some sense," as Anita always says. As a pharmacist, Anita carried me financially while I completed my studies to become a pharmacist. After obtaining my degree, I started working 16 hours a day to provide for my family. After receiving the Lord into my life at the age of 30, I realized that He provided for His own even whilst they sleep (Psalm 127:2), and this restored balance to my life.

Soon after we started a new business venture in the hearing-aid field, temptation nearly got the better of me. I always tell our children that temptation does not come in the form of a beautiful lady walking down the street in a red suit and a fork in her hand. That would be too obvious.

Temptation comes when you least expect it. It comes via the person you work with daily, and plan and discuss various aspects of business over a cup of coffee. It comes when you pray together for a new venture and for each other. Gradually, spiritual closeness leads to sexual awareness—a massive snare, ready to destroy everything in its way: relationships, marriages, companies, churches, people and, most importantly, your relationship with God.

If I had known what heartache, tears and stress this would cause in my relationship with Anita for many years, I would not have been so naïve. I would have avoided the snare of emotional entanglement.

Two verses constantly mulled through my mind during this time: The first was, "For the Lord, the God of Israel, says he hates divorce and cruel men. Therefore control your passions—let there be no divorcing of your wives" (Malachi 2:16), and the second, "And you husbands, show the same kind of love to your wives as Christ showed to the Church when he died for her …" (Ephesians 5:25).

At times, I cried, "Lord, it's difficult!"—just to be answered by the Holy Spirit, "You *must* love your wife." In sheer desperation, I cried out one day, "Lord, if I must love my wife, I want You to help me; I can't do it on my own." The most amazing thing happened. When I decided to give our marriage another chance, the Lord's power manifested in our relationship and the Holy Spirit re-ignited a new spark of love for Anita.

Things started to change and I looked at Anita through different eyes. I developed an appreciation for her that I never had before. I saw how special and talented she was, and I became aware that I would have made the biggest mistake of my life had I chosen the broad instead of the narrow way.

One morning during my quiet time, a few years later, it dawned on me that I had never asked Anita's forgiveness for the pain and heartache I had caused her. I went into the bedroom, sat on the bed next to her and asked her to forgive me. I made no excuses, nor tried to explain or justify my actions. She forgave me, and from that day real healing set in and our relationship changed for the better. Her frankness—which attracted me at the beginning of our relationship and then gradually started irritating me—again became something I could appreciate and love her for, especially after reading Proverbs 24:26: "It is an honor to receive a frank reply."

Long before my emotional entanglement, Anita and I discussed what to do if we ever took a wrong business decision and stared bankruptcy in the face. I will never forget her words: "We can both work hard and if the Lord blesses us with good health, we can live in a tent in the trailer park and start from scratch."

I know of very few wives who will support their husbands to the bitter end, even if it means living in a tent. From that day onwards, I made a willful decision to consult Anita regarding both the big and small decisions in our company, as she was prepared to sacrifice all. As the apostle Paul says, "… a man is really doing himself a favor and loving himself when he loves his wife!" (Ephesians 5:28b).

I also realized that one must choose to make the right and godly decision *before* encountering the temptation. Two extracts from my daily devotionals were especially apt: "I have promised that for every day you live, the strength shall be given to you. Do not fear." [4] I realized that although I might doubt my own strength to resist, God promises to intervene if the occasion arises.

"Your heart is a fertile greenhouse ready to produce good fruit. Your mind is the doorway to your heart—the strategic place where you determine which seeds are sown and which seeds are discarded. The Holy Spirit is ready to help manage and filter the thoughts that try and enter. He can help you guard your heart … He stands with you on the threshold. A thought approaches, a questionable thought. Do you throw open the door and let it enter? Of course not. You 'fight to capture every thought until it acknowledges the authority of Christ' (2 Corinthians 10:5 Phillips). You don't leave the door unguarded." [5]

When I read this last sentence, I saw my hand reaching out to the door and "locking" my heart. At that moment, I grasped the importance of locking one's heart to questionable thoughts and thereby remaining faithful to one's spouse. By performing this simple act before encountering temptation, the decision is actually already made. Delaying the decision and *hoping* to make the right one in the heat of the moment may have disastrous consequences.

Ask God to help you resist your temptations. Our responsibility is to guard our minds and our hearts at all cost and to trust Him for the strength to resist when it is needed. While guarding our minds and our hearts, we also have the responsibility to avoid, and steer away from tempting situations.

Materialism

In his book, *The Man in the Mirror*, Patrick Morley makes the following profound statement: "No test of a man's true character is more conclusive than how he spends his time and his money." [6]

Materialism is such an important topic that I decided to devote a whole chapter to it (see "Closing the Circle"). Does this mean that we are not to buy anything? Of course not. Proverbs is replete with pointers on the need to work hard and save our earnings: "... wealth from hard work grows" (Proverbs 13:11b); "Quick wealth is not a blessing in the end" (Proverbs 20:21); "Steady plodding brings prosperity; hasty speculation brings poverty" (Proverbs 21:5); "The wise man saves for the future, but the foolish man spends whatever he gets" (Proverbs 21:20); and so forth.

Materialism and greed often go hand-in-hand. It certainly resulted in the credit crisis of 2008–2010. So often we feel everybody else is successful and getting ahead, while we are left behind. Not true! Our neighborhood is filled with "For Sale" signs everywhere. Gone are the boats, the SUVs and the quad-bikes ... Did we really need all these material things, or should we rather have saved for tougher times? My heart goes out to the poor who were misled by unscrupulous bankers or financial advisors into accepting mortgages they could not afford. Driven by financial institutions' greed, the poor now have to pay.

Proverbs 23:4–5 warns, "Don't weary yourself trying to get rich. Why waste your time? For riches can disappear as though they had the wings of a bird!" And yet, Proverbs 12:14 also states that if we tell the truth and work hard, many blessings will be returned to us.

I constantly have to remind myself not to strive for that which I do not have, and that I will gather my riches little by little, one step at a time. One of my staff members often reminds me of Proverbs 13:11: "Dishonest money dwindles away, but he who gathers money little by little makes it grow" (NIV).

Materialism often leads to a debt trap—enslaving us to financial institutions for as long as we walk this earth. Once we refrain from falling into the trap of constantly upgrading (homes, cars, computers and other worldly goods) and buying things we do not really need, we'll have discretionary income that will release us of our debt and we'll be able to help those less fortunate than we are. Only then will we be able to put aside our own desires and be in a position to help others.

James touches on the subject of materialism when he writes, "What is causing the quarrels and fights among you? Isn't it because there is a whole army of evil desires within you? You want what you don't have, so you kill to get it. You long for what others have, and can't afford it, so you start a fight to take it away from them. And yet the reason you don't have what you want is that you don't ask God for it. And even when you do ask you don't get it because your whole aim is wrong—you want only what will give you pleasure" (James 4:1–3).

The apostle Peter also gives sound advice: "Next, learn to put aside your own desires so that you will become patient and godly, gladly letting God have his way with you. This will make possible the next step, which is for you to enjoy other people and to like them, and finally you will grow to love them deeply. The more you go on in this way, the more you will grow strong spiritually and become fruitful and useful to our Lord Jesus Christ. But anyone who fails to go after these additions to faith is blind indeed, or at least very shortsighted, and has forgotten that God delivered him from the old life of sin so that now he can live a strong, good life for the Lord" (2 Peter 1:6–8).

Let us look at this Scripture from a practical perspective. How do people and companies respond in tough times? Companies mostly retrench staff to protect their bottom line. Is this a blessing or a curse?

If I need to set aside my own desires and take Peter's warning to heart, then surely my first responsibility in times of adversity should be to look after the wellbeing of those the Lord has entrusted to my care, before even looking after my shareholders or myself. This implies becoming a blessing rather than a curse to my fellow men. Surely, I should dig deep into my reserves and help those who are unable to help themselves. And yet, we see people losing their homes while bankers pay themselves bonuses for a job well done!

Entire communities are affected by companies retrenching workers in order to protect the bottom line. Should we not avoid investing in companies that fire employees in tough times under the pretence of cost-cutting? Surely a culture of saving should be encouraged during good times, so that bad times can be managed in a godly manner? Remember the seven fat years and the seven lean years in Egypt—or is there so much pressure on performance, bonuses, quarterly results and unrealistic growth that everything is sacrificed for the sake of the bottom line?

This, of course, applies to all of us! Is materialism—the magnetic power of instant gratification—so strong that we are prepared to beg, borrow and steal in order to obtain that which we yearn for, and yet regard as worthless in difficult times?

Author John Piper defines covetousness as "… desiring something so much that you lose your contentment in God. The opposite of covetousness is contentment in God." He adds, " … covetousness is a heart divided between two gods." [7]

According to the apostle Paul, covetousness is synonymous with idolatry: "Put to death, therefore, whatever belongs to your earthly nature: sexual immorality, impurity, lust, evil desires and greed, which is idolatry" (Colossians 3:5–6 NIV).

As Christians, we should avoid this trap of materialism and the debt we incur to support our yearnings and lust for things at any cost. Ask God for His assistance when wanting to make unnecessary purchases. It is amazing how the things I absolutely crave and simply have to have, tend to lose their luster as time goes by.

Pride

Proverbs 8:13 cautions, "If anybody respects and fears God, he will hate evil. For wisdom hates pride, arrogance, corruption and deceit of every kind."

John Piper emphasizes that "... covetousness is turning away from God, usually to find satisfaction in things ... that lust is turning away from God to find satisfaction in sex ... that bitterness is turning away from God to find satisfaction in revenge ... that impatience is turning away from God to find satisfaction in your own uninterrupted plan of action ... that anxiety, misplaced shame, and despondency are various conditions of the heart when these efforts of unbelief miscarry."

He adds, "But deeper than all these forms of unbelief is the unbelief of pride, because self-determination and self-exaltation lie behind all these other sinful dispositions. Every turning from God—for anything—presumes a kind of autonomy or independence that is the essence of pride. Turning from God assumes that one knows better than God. Thus pride lies at the root of every turning from God. It is the root of every act of distrust toward God." [8]

Pride causes us to want recognition. It makes us take too much or full credit for our achievements and is often the result of wealth, too much power and self-righteousness. It interferes with our ability to reason. It keeps us from asking others for help. It causes us to judge others and keeps us from admitting our sins. It affects our relationships and keeps us blind to our own faults. It is also often a barrier to believing in Jesus.

Lessons in Humility

Someone once said, "Humility is not belittling of the self. It is forgetting self, because you are remembering the Lord."

After doing some market research in the nineties, I devised a "facts" advertising campaign for our company, which included interviews with certain user groups. According to the campaign, our products were "the most sought after, gave the best performance and service, were the most widely recognized", etc, etc. Anita did not approve and warned me that the campaign came across as "arrogant". I disregarded her well-meant advice and continued with the campaign.

Complaints began rolling in soon after the first advertisements appeared. I was called in to explain the campaign to the Executive Committee of the Professional Society of which I was a member. I was fired up and ready to prove my stance—and to point out the skeletons in their own cupboards! Shortly before the meeting, the Lord woke me at two o'clock one morning. It was a night I will never forget. God "wiped the floor with me" that night and showed me the sin of pride in my life. I begged for forgiveness, immediately withdrew the campaign, apologized to the Committee and vowed never to run such a campaign again.

I remember arriving back at the office after the meeting, feeling lousy. I shared this with my personal assistant. After all, I expected to feel elated after having acknowledged my mistake. Her blunt response was, "How can you expect to feel good? You *should* feel lousy after what you've done." Her words put everything into perspective—a difficult, but worthwhile lesson in humility.

How we need to guard our strengths, or they will become a double weakness. In Proverbs 30:7–9, Agur begs two favors from God: "First, help me never to tell a lie. Second, give me neither poverty nor riches! Give me just enough to satisfy my needs! For if I grow rich, I may become content without God. And if I am too poor, I may steal, and thus insult God's holy name."

I had a friend with whom I prayed for five years. During that time, he often said unflattering things about his senior partner, someone I knew. Instead of verifying the facts, I believed him. I later employed him, as he told me that the company in which he held a small share was sold out from under him by his senior partner and that he was left with nothing. Again, I believed him without checking the facts.

We opened our home, our hearts and our business to this friend. We shared everything with him, including our company know-how. After 14 months, a staff member brought to my attention that he was busy setting up his own company in opposition to ours. When I confronted him, he denied it categorically. He did, however, leave our employ soon after and started up his own company. In hindsight, this man tried to destroy the excellent relationship I had with my son, Nico Junior, and Pieta, my son-in-law, both directors and senior managers in our company.

In a letter to him, I expressed my concerns regarding his sincerity as a Christian—not because of starting a business in opposition to us, but the manner in which he had gone about it. During the months before his departure, he made an in-depth study of our company, our clients and our systems, and in addition, recruited some of our staff.

A few months later, my friend Gerrit said that while praying for me, the Lord laid it upon his heart to tell me to read Isaiah 58:1–10. I still recall him being very apologetic about it, saying, "My brother, I know you live your life like this, yet, I feel compelled to pass it on." I read the Scripture and when I came to verse 9, I immediately felt this related in some way to the person who had left our employ: "Then when you call, the Lord will answer, 'Yes I am here,' he will quickly reply. All you need to do is to stop oppressing the weak, and to stop making false accusations and spreading vicious rumors!"

For one thing, I had to stop talking about how much we had done for him and how he had repaid us. On the other hand, I felt compelled to make an appointment with his ex-partner and ask for his forgiveness for having believed the lies I had been told about him. During our meeting, he said, "Had I known that this man started working for you, I would have contacted you and warned you about my experiences with him and the millions he had cost our company."

From the uncomfortable starting point of having to ask for forgiveness, a close friendship evolved. Subsequently, his Foundation became a major donor to our school. Had pride withheld me from humbling myself before him, I would have lost the opportunity to befriend this man of tremendous integrity and gain a trusted brother in Christ.

We have always made use of a very nice guesthouse near our company for visitors. We once entertained some Swiss visitors and arranged a typical South African barbeque at the guesthouse for 10 people. The food was mediocre and when I received the bill a few days later, I became angry as the amount exceeded what we had originally agreed upon, due to petty additional charges. I decided to pay the bill and never to support them again.

Two years later, while sitting in church and on the point of enjoying Holy Communion, the pastor mentioned that anyone who was aware of some unforgiveness in their heart should not participate in the Communion, but should first go and set the matter right, lest they ate and drank a curse on themselves (1 Corinthians 11:29). I immediately thought about the owner of the guesthouse and my boycotting of his establishment. I decided not to take Communion until I had the opportunity to talk to him.

I made an appointment and went to see him. I asked him to forgive me for not having brought my unhappiness to his attention and for avoiding his establishment ever since. He was utterly surprised and said, "If only you had told me, we could have discussed the matter—and of course, I forgive you." We enjoyed a cup of coffee together and the morning I had dreaded, turned into a blessing. Even more amazing is that this guesthouse owner subsequently also started supporting our school financially from time to time.

Had pride withheld me from humbling myself and asking this man's forgiveness, my spiritual life would have suffered. Unforgiveness is a self-inflicted prison.

In his book, *Grace for the Moment*, Max Lucado quotes 1 Peter 2:20: "If you suffer for doing good, and you are patient, then God is pleased." He elaborates on the unwillingness to forgive, stating, "Is there any emotion that imprisons the soul more than the unwillingness to forgive? What do you do when people mistreat you or those you love? Does the fire of anger boil within you, with leaping flames consuming your emotions? Or do you reach somewhere, to some source of cool water and pull out a bucket of mercy—to free yourself?

"Don't get on the roller coaster of resentment and anger. You be the one who says, 'Yes, he mistreated me, but I am going to be like Christ. I'll be the one who says 'Forgive them, Father, they don't know what they're doing.'" [9]

Forgiving my father for what he had done to my mother and to us as a family was probably one of the most difficult things I've ever had to do. The Lord showed me in a miraculous way, through a dream, that I was not to judge him, because I did not know anything about his past or the abuse, suffering and rejection he experienced as a child.

I was to love him unconditionally and accept him wholeheartedly. He had dinner with us one evening, and I distinctly remember saying to him, "Dad, I would like you to know that I love you very much." A difficult statement then, but I knew I had to express forgiveness in love if I wanted to experience peace.

I will never forget the look in his eyes, as he probably had not heard these words in many, many years. I felt an immense relief and freedom from the chains of unforgiveness, which had kept me in bondage for so many years. After a short illness, he passed away a few years later and I had no regrets for leaving things unsaid.

I realized that forgiving people, no matter what they have done to you, is a biblical principle and God will reward you for it. I always remember Jesus' prayer: "And forgive our sins—for we have forgiven those who sinned against us" (Luke 11:4a).

Many people harbor unforgiveness in their hearts due to some form of abuse they suffered as children at the hands of adults—often parents, teachers, family members and friends. Perhaps one of the most hidden of secrets is that of mothers having sexually molested their sons. I have spoken to a number of men who endured this form of abuse as young boys, but pride and shame withheld them from even admitting it to themselves for many years, let alone dealing with the devastating effects.

Only once we are able to deal with issues by the grace of God, will we be able to offer forgiveness and be released from the bondage experienced for so many years. Often, professional help by godly counselors is necessary to peel back the layers of shame, unforgiveness and guilt in order for us to be set free.

CHAPTER 8

CLOSING THE CIRCLE

Jesus said ...

*"'Don't store up treasures here on
earth where they can
erode away or may be stolen.
Store them in heaven where they will never
lose their value,
and are safe from thieves.
If your profits are in heaven your heart
will be there too.'"*

(Matthew 6:19–21)

*"'You cannot serve two masters: God and money.
For you will hate one and love the other, or else
the other way around.'"*

(Matthew 6:24)

Upgrading versus Downgrading

I am writing this account in the midst of one of the most extensive economic crises in living memory, so perhaps it is time to share some thoughts on how I "closed my circle", or as some would call it, "capped my lifestyle".

According to a recent newspaper report, the average white South African changes homes 7.2 times in his or her lifetime. An interesting statement, especially in view of the fact that we rarely downgrade and nearly always upgrade. Upgrading usually goes hand-in-hand with borrowing more as the family income increases and as banks offer home-owners larger amounts of money based on the strength of their income and the value of the new (or old) home.

And so, we enslave ourselves to the banks and subject ourselves to interest rate hikes, which in our country can be anything between 10% and 26% depending on the economy, the value of our currency and the inflation rate. In addition, we are offered 20- and even 30-year repayment periods with access bond facilities, also known as "home equity loans". Thus, we remain in debt. Add car repayments, school and university fees, medical insurance and taxes, and very little if anything remains after all our debts are paid and obligations met. Not surprisingly, many Christians have little to give to the church and even less to the poor, as they slave away month after month to make ends meet.

Is this really what God intended for His children? Proverbs 3:9–10 emphasizes, "Honor the Lord by giving him the first part of all your income, and he will fill your barns with wheat and barley and overflow your wine vats with the finest wines."

Surely, this means that we should honor the Lord with our "first fruits" (our tithes) and contribute to His work with a glad and joyful heart. The apostle Paul underscores the fact that " … cheerful givers are the ones God prizes" (2 Corinthians 9:7b). In turn, He promises to "fill our barns and overflow our wine vats". Overflowing implies having enough to share with others as God's Word directs us: fellow Christians going through difficult times, as well as the poor. Surplus income should therefore not be directed at upgrading our standard of living or becoming self-indulgent. Why then are so many Christians not enjoying this wonderful promise of overflowing vats? Why do so many Christians struggle from month-end to month-end?

Years ago, Gerrit and I discussed this issue and looked at the pros and cons. We discussed the pressure of a modern lifestyle and the culture of instant gratification, enhanced by the availability of easy credit for "wants" rather than "needs". We also discussed what we would do with a gift of a million dollars, and what we would do if God intended us to pass it on to someone else. Would our own needs be so extensive that hardly a cent would be passed on? What was required for God to entrust us with this amount, or more? Would it merely be a gift to be passed on to a person or an organization? Unfair question? Give it some thought: When will you be able to pass on that which was not intended for you in the first place?

We concluded that the answer lies in making a willful decision to cap one's lifestyle, close one's circle, avoid the trap of continuously upgrading by moving from one house to an even larger one, and from one fancy car to the next. In other words, *being content with what we have* is the key.

In his letter to the Philippians, Paul says, "I know how to live on almost nothing or with everything. I have learned the secret of contentment in every situation, whether it be a full stomach or hunger, plenty or want; for I can do everything God asks me to with the help of Christ who gives me the strength and power" (Philippians 4:12-13).

I must confess that the Lord blessed me with a wife who kept me from moving from bigger to better to best. By remaining in the same house we purchased in 1975, we were able to give our children the stability they would never otherwise have known had we moved incessantly.

I wish I could share with you in person the freedom experienced when you cap your lifestyle, and in so doing, become debt free. "Impossible," you might say, but I am convinced that it is within the reach of every person. Being content with *what you have* and with *who you are* is possible.

In his book, *Debt-Free Living*, Larry Burkett says that regardless of how it seems today, debt is abnormal in any economy and should not be normal in the eyes of God's people. We live in a debt-ridden society, now virtually dependent on a constant expansion of credit to keep the economy going.[1]

The first edition of Burkett's book was published in 1999. Now, more than a decade later, this statement still rings true. The joy of closing your circle and capping your lifestyle is that you no longer need to keep up with the Joneses. It is easier than you may think, and once implemented, will afford so much financial freedom, you will never want to incur debt again or revert to your old ways.

I have shared this principle with my children, friends and acquaintances; trust me, it is life-changing. Once you are financially free, you will have money to enjoy and to share with those in need. Being generous with your possessions is a true act of love towards our fellowmen, but more importantly, it pleases God.

In his book, *Money, Possessions and Eternity*, Randy Alcorn advocates a simple lifestyle and says that in biblical terms, "The rich are not told they must take a vow of poverty. They are told essentially to take a vow of generosity. They are to be rich in good deeds, quick to share, and quick to part with their assets for kingdom causes. In doing so, they will lay up treasures in heaven." [2]

How can I lay up treasures in heaven? Surely, I cannot give what I do not have. Exactly! If we have monthly commitments pertaining to house, car and credit card installments, how can we be generous and quick to share if we have very little or nothing left? The answer lies in a debt-free lifestyle. This, in turn, is only possible by capping our lifestyle. I have tried it, my children have tried it and friends have tried it—and it works. Take responsibility, stop blaming others, and start making the right decisions.

Five Steps to Financial Freedom

I would like to share with you a simple five-step plan to financial freedom:

Step One: Pray

Pray about your current financial situation and ask God what He would prefer for your lifestyle. Ask Him for wisdom regarding what to put inside the circle, and to work in the hearts of your spouse and children so that they too may realize the need to cap their lifestyles. Pray for the strength and courage to be able to close your circle and withstand the temptation of breaking the circle with some unnecessary luxury.

For me, Romans 12:2 reaffirms this line of thinking: "Don't copy the behavior and customs of this world, but be a new and different person with a fresh newness in all you do and think. Then you will learn from your own experience how his ways will really satisfy you."

Step Two: Plan

Before you can become debt free, you need to decide on the non-negotiable, absolute "must haves" in your circle before closing it. Start your financial planning by listing things you would like to see in the circle. Then eliminate the "nice to haves". Among other, my "must haves" include tithes, shelter, food, clothing, transport, education, health care, and relaxation (vacations).

This could turn into a very interesting family discussion. Debating about the "non-negotiables" or the "very important needs" can be quite insightful. It may mean getting rid of the junk and "nice to haves" (which invariably cost money to maintain) versus saving for the children's college education. The objective of this exercise is not to allocate the family income to the last cent, but to eliminate everything unnecessary. While the idea is to free the family of debt as quickly as possible, bear in mind that every family is unique. Therefore, do not compare yourself with anybody else.

Planning is a biblical principle according to Proverbs 16:9: "We should make plans—counting on God to direct us." Always remember, "A wise man thinks ahead; a fool doesn't, and even brags about it!" (Proverbs 13:16).

It should be clear to anyone that if you don't plan for the future, there will be no future. This exercise may take a few days or even some weeks to complete. Part of the strategy should not only be to cut costs, but also to look at supplementing your income—but *not* at your family's expense. Working overtime and weekends, or getting a second or third job for extended periods of time will result in neglecting your family, which is not the godly thing to do.

Consider all the options, even the ones that are not all that obvious. Perhaps you can rent out the spare room, or convert the garage into a small apartment, or help out at a local store on Saturdays—all of which can generate extra income. Generating extra income and cutting costs will soon improve your financial situation.

Before I became a Christian, I used to work seven days a week from eight in the morning to eleven o'clock at night to provide for my family. I worked in our own pharmacy during the day and in a friend's after-hour pharmacy at night. This continued for six years. Shortly after my conversion, I read Psalm 127:1–3 and suddenly realized that I was not trusting in the Lord to provide: "Unless the Lord builds a house, the builders' work is useless. Unless the Lord protects a city, sentries do no good. It is senseless for you to work so hard from early morning until late at night, fearing you will starve to death; for God wants his loved ones to get their proper rest."

I summarily resigned from my night duties and to this day, I am reminded of the Lord's provision as I walk into my office in the morning and see the orders faxed through during the night. The Lord is still keeping to His promise of years ago: If I love and follow Him, He will provide, even while I sleep.

Here are some suggestions to assist you in your financial planning and discussions:

- Start by listing those things you would like to see in your circle. Every family member should be given the opportunity to draw their own circle, but ultimately, there should only be one circle for the entire family.

List your income and expenditure, and remove or sell those items that are not absolutely necessary. Continue with this exercise until you've cut your expenses to the bone.

• Any surplus funds should be utilized to pay off your debt. You will be amazed at how an extra couple of dollars a month will reduce the number of years over which you have to pay off your home loan or mortgage. Utilize bonuses to pay off your debt. The family's main goal should be to become debt free as rapidly and as effectively as possible. Perhaps that special vacation can be thrown in as a reward, once the target of being debt free is met?

• Contributing to your local church and/or missionaries should form part of this discussion. Tithing, the giving of your "first fruits", is most important and should be placed right at the top of your monthly expense list. So often, the stress and pressure of high debt levels cause us to cut or eliminate that which is our first and most important obligation. Giving to God what is due to Him is critically important. Not being able to tithe equates to stealing from God.

• A family home close to schools and in a good suburb may be one need. (See debt reduction below.) You might live in a less than favorable suburb with crime on the rise, or where a highway is projected in the vicinity. If so, put a new home inside your circle. This should only be done once the positives and the negatives, as well as the affordability of a new home have been discussed in detail.

• A family car (or cars) is usually a sensitive topic. Dad often wants a car for "show" (we are after all successful, you know!) and Mom might want a more practical car to taxi the children around. But do you really need a car, Dad, if you are within walking distance from your job, or are able to make use of public transport? If you drive a standard car now, be careful not to want to upgrade to a more luxurious vehicle, such as the most expensive SUV. By curbing your lifestyle, you have to stay with a specific class of vehicle, unless your needs (not your wants) change.

- Consider the quality and quantity of your food. Is it really necessary to buy at the most expensive stores or delicatessens, or enjoy a meal at only the best restaurants? Is it really necessary to have a starter, main course, dessert and the finest wines when you go out for a meal?

- The children's college education must also be planned and placed in the circle. We all want our children to go to the very best colleges or universities, but is this really necessary? Can you really afford it without becoming debt-ridden, or even worse, burdening your children with study debt? Surely, living at home is far more affordable and cost-effective than living on a college campus?

- "Nice to have" items like quad-bikes, boats, computer games, elaborate holidays, designer clothes, lavish parties, first- or business-class flying and other big-ticket items may have to go once you start saving for your children's education, or that planned family holiday. What may be important to one family might not be important or applicable to another. Every family is unique and has its own needs, desires and priorities. What might sound extravagant to one could be completely normal to another. Disregard what other families deem essential and look prayerfully at your own situation. Anyway, the Joneses went belly-up long ago, because they lived in debt and spent more than they earned in their quest for instant gratification.

Step Three: Implement

After you have prayerfully planned your finances and selected the indispensable items to put inside your circle, including any possible future necessities, start implementing your plan. Plan your work and work your plan. Whatever you do, close your circle, cap your lifestyle and reduce your debt!

Needless to say, the whole family must work together as a team with regular updates on events and attitudes. A debt barometer in the kitchen could also keep every member of the household focused on the goal. As debt decreases, everyone will be encouraged to do more. Family members will soon realize that, once the house and cars are paid for, there may be no need to incur debt for the children's studies, or that long-awaited vacation.

The main focus of wanting to become debt free should ultimately be to do more for others. Living debt free actually frees up money that would otherwise have gone to financial institutions for virtually a lifetime (20 to 30 years!) in order to cover our installments. Imagine this money going to more worthy causes as we give freely and generously, not only to others, but also to our family as and when the need arises.

This is a biblical instruction according to Ephesians 4:28: "If anyone is stealing he must stop it and begin using those hands of his for honest work so he can give to others in need."

Author Randy Alcorn says, "We should work not only to care for our families and because it's healthy, but also so that we can take the excess income and use it to help the needy." [3] Being burdened with debt, often incurred "for our family's sake", keeps us impoverished and enslaved to the banks.

The trick is not to fall back into the debt trap once you have accumulated surplus cash. Therefore, when implementing the above, take into account what you have to do to get out of debt, preferably within six years. Why six years? In biblical times, when a person could not repay his debt within this period of time, he was released of his debt on the premise that he would not be able to pay his debt anyway. This might be a very ambitious goal for some, but if you do not plan on becoming debt free, you never will.

Once debt free, you will be amazed at the freedom you will experience. Adverse events like interest rate fluctuations, stock market slumps, tight liquidity cycles, broken washing machines, unexpected home repairs, and so on, will no longer be of concern, but they will certainly have a large impact if you are over-extended in terms of your finances.

Step Four: Save

Proverbs 21:20 states, "The wise man saves for the future, but the foolish man spends whatever he gets."

Once you are debt free, saving and investing part of the surplus cash you now have should form an integral part of your strategy. Our family has a number of legal investment trusts to protect our wealth against the country's high estate duties and capital gains tax. As a family, we plan our investment strategies in a manner that is always mindful of our most important and largest commitment: our investment in the kingdom of God. As someone once said, "Our standard of giving should increase, not our standard of living."

As a family, we determine the amounts to be given for God's cause, the vision the Lord gave me (see chapter on "Vision"), and for the needy. In a third world country there are endless needs. Although the poor will always be with us, I cannot allow myself the luxury of becoming discouraged. Every day, I have to make a difference to those the Lord sends across my path. No more and no less—I cannot turn a blind eye to the needs God brings to my attention, and at the same time proclaim my love for Christ. Generosity is a biblical principle: "If God has given you money, be generous in helping others with it" (Romans 12:8b).

I am aware of the fact that it is probably easier for our family to decide how to cap our lifestyle and where to give, as we all work in the same family business. It might not be as easy if your children have their own jobs. But let us learn from the families with so-called "old money". They normally have conservative lifestyles and grow the family wealth to benefit many. Is it really necessary for every family member to have his/her own vacation home, mountain cabin or ski lodge? Why does the family not share, thus allowing everyone to enjoy these luxuries together? In this way, the whole family will become debt free much quicker, without necessarily sacrificing luxuries such as a vacation home. By doing this, we will also free up money to generously meet the requirements of the needy.

Above all, let us seek simplicity in all things. Why upgrade if we only need to renovate? During the 35 years we have lived in our home, we have added, renovated and painted a number of times, and each time our house felt brand new. By doing this, we have saved tens of thousands in moving, upgrading, paying property and government taxes, as well as bank costs.

If we drive a quality car, why change it every few years merely to drive a new model? We implemented the practice of good stewardship by handing down cars to family or staff, rather than buying new ones and selling older ones at a loss. In so doing, we have kept new vehicle purchases to a minimum.

Once you start living debt free, you will be amazed at how your thinking changes. I used to fly business class on domestic flights, while I still owed the bank money. Since becoming debt free, the whole family travels economy class on budget airlines. But, we no longer drive 1,000 miles to our holiday home; we fly to Cape Town and rent a car. Our traveling patterns have become a non-negotiable as a direct result of our debt-free living and our capped lifestyle. Our whole family drives safe, smaller cars, because there is no longer any need for a large car for long-distance trips.

Step Five: Give

The best way to fight greed is to give. I give away money, clothes (I have a weakness for nice jackets, but then end up giving them to my friends or staff), blankets, cars, vacations and the like—as the need arises. But, my first priority is to tithe as we are reminded in God's Word: "You must tithe all of your crops every year. Bring this tithe to eat before the Lord your God at the place he shall choose as his sanctuary; this applies to your tithes of grain, new wine, olive oil, and the firstborn of your flocks and herds. The

purpose of tithing is to teach you always to put God first in your lives" *
(Deuteronomy 14:22–23).

In addition, I also have to take care of the needs of my "extended
family", which includes 230 employees. Our family has an active plan in
respect of giving, and this includes giving generously to the Lord's cause
and those in need. As a family, we primarily support the cause of the deaf
and the expansion of God's kingdom. You may find that you would like to
invest in something else. Pray about it and ask God to show you where
you should channel your surplus time and money after tithing.

Isaiah 58:3–11 has always played a major role in considering our
employees, the people the Lord entrusted to our company. Ensuring
that we have adequate reserves to carry the company and our
employees during trying times is important and only possible when the
shareholders (our family) have realistic expectations and a capped lifestyle.
Precautionary measures must be in place in order to protect the jobs of
those who have been loyal and hardworking, especially during difficult
times.

I cannot over-emphasize the importance of this Scripture. When
I initially read it, it had a profound impact on my thought and decision-
making processes. I prayed about it, made it my own, and implemented
what it said. We have since looked after our employees to the best of our
ability, we have tried to feed the hungry and the poor, we have tried to
help those in trouble and we have not shied away from family members
who needed our help. We have never given it much thought; we have just
done it. By implementing these basic principles, we have been blessed in
our business, in our homes, in our families and above all else, in our spirit. In
addition, we have a more meaningful relationship with Jesus.

Part of our giving also goes to edifying those in full-time ministry. For
the past 20 years, our family has had the privilege of supporting the Grace
Ministers' Conferences in South Africa. These conferences are specifically

---

* Farmers in the central part of our country have taken tithing to a new level. When they deliver
their grain or maize crops to the silos, they immediately earmark 10% of their crops to their local
church's account. By bringing their first crops to the Lord, they avoid the temptation of spending
the money once it reaches their bank accounts.

held for hundreds of pastors and their wives at the beginning of each year to spiritually equip and prepare them for the year ahead. Bible teachers from all over the world, mainly from the USA, provide valuable input at these events.

The conference is held at a beautiful four-star lodge in the mountains near Johannesburg and special rates are negotiated as the conference is held during the first or second week of each year—traditionally a slack period for conferences. What a blessing to hear the testimonies of men of God who arrive discouraged and leave infused by the Word of God, excited about God's plan for them and their congregations. We could not have asked for a better return on our investment!

According to Isaiah 23:18, it is our duty to see that our pastors are well cared for and that they earn at least the average annual income of the congregation's members: "Yet [the distant time will come when] her businesses will give their profits to the Lord! They will not be hoarded but used for good food and fine clothes for the priests of the Lord!" This is only possible when we have a capped lifestyle and a spirit of generosity.

I wish to reiterate that for me the most effective way of fighting greed in my own life is to give my money away. And yes, "It is possible to give away and become richer! It is also possible to hold on too tightly and lose everything. Yes, the liberal man shall be rich! By watering others, he waters himself" (Proverbs 11:24–25).

Proverbs 11:28 has also helped me not to put my trust in money, but rather in God: "Trust in your money and down you go! Trust in God and flourish as a tree!"

Some people have bought large houses, cars, equities and savings with tithes that should have gone to the Lord's house, only to see the value diminish overnight, together with the banks they trusted so much.

Malachi 3:8–11 warns, "'Will a man rob God? Surely not! And yet you have robbed me ... You have robbed me of the tithes and offerings due to me ... Bring all the tithes into the storehouse so that there will be food enough in my Temple; if you do, I will open up the windows of heaven for you and pour out a blessing so great you won't have room enough to take it in! Try it! Let me prove it to you! Your crops will be large, for I will guard them from insects and plagues. Your grapes won't shrivel away before they ripen,' says the Lord Almighty."

Had we given our tithes, and everything else collapsed around us, we at least would have had one rock-solid investment.

Helping the poor is a constant theme throughout the Bible. Proverbs 19:17 says, "When you help the poor you are lending to the Lord—and he pays wonderful interest on your loan!" This is reiterated in Proverbs 21:13: "He who shuts his ears to the cries of the poor will be ignored in his own time of need." And again in Galatians 2:10: "The only thing they did suggest was that we must always remember to help the poor, and I [Paul], too, was eager for that."

I have witnessed so-called Christian businessmen in Nigeria playing loud spiritual songs in their cars, but having no compassion for the poor. Their ungracious acts towards the poor made me realize that as Christians we must be doers of the Word and not listeners only. James 2:17 puts this truth into perspective: "So you see, it isn't enough just to have faith. You must also do good to prove that you have it. Faith that doesn't show itself by good works is no faith at all—it is dead and useless."

At times, I have had to devise ways and means to help the poor, including widows and orphans. I often still get caught up in meeting my own needs first without giving thought to the needs of others, and every so often, the Lord taps me on the shoulder to remind me of my "other commitments".

Spurgeon says, "We can do more by care than by cash, and most with the two together" [4] In other words, it will be far more profitable for me to become unselfish, and out of love for the Lord Jesus begin to care for the souls of those around me.

Psalm 41:1–3 gives us a wonderful promise of blessing if we help the poor: "God blesses those who are kind to the poor. He helps them out of their troubles. He protects them and keeps them alive; he publicly honors them and destroys the power of their enemies. He nurses them when they are sick, and soothes their pains and worries."

Debt-free Living

Once you have experienced the freedom of debt-free living, you will inevitably become stress free and you will never want to turn back again. Yes, you may live in a smaller house or apartment, drive a smaller car and eat out less, but you will have peace at heart, you will have money in the bank, and on the day you must write out a check for some or other worthy cause, you will be amazed at the size of the check you'll be able to write.

At this stage, you may want to ask some questions:

1. What about vacations, hobbies and eating out?

Once debt free, one can of course pursue these items in moderation. Author Randy Alcorn clarifies it as follows: "There's nothing wrong with spending money for modest pleasures that renew and revive us, especially considering that our battle will last a lifetime. I'm grateful to have fun possessions, such as a bicycle and tennis racket. They aren't necessary; yet they contribute to my physical and mental health. Our family spends money on vacations that aren't 'necessary,' yet they bring renewal and precious relationship-building opportunities. My wife and I sometimes go out to dinner, enriching our relationship and renewing our vigor to return to life's battles. We can give away much or most of our income yet still have breathing room for legitimate recreational spending." [5]

2. What about saving for retirement?

Let me ask you a question: Where in the Bible does it say that anyone retired? I once wished to retire at 50, just to find that I was putting my whole life on hold. Once I realized the foolishness of this, I started *living*! I have saved for my retirement since my first paycheck, as it has always been considered the right thing to do. At times, that money would have meant a lot to my young family, only to find that—due to inflation and economic downturns—the amount that was eventually paid out, did not even equate to 10% of that which was promised 35 years ago!

To work for as long as you can, reduces the need for retirement and alleviates the stress of not being able to get by once you retire. When I see the scores of retired Americans still working, albeit in different jobs than those they retired from, they are an example to the many people around the world who wish that they could retire, just to sit on the patio, play golf or simply do nothing. Why do we not copy the American model of actively creating jobs in our communities and companies, specifically reserved for retired people?

The Lord provided for our whole family way beyond our expectations and in the most unexpected ways. We prayerfully made certain business decisions, such as purchasing properties for some of our offices around the country due to the high rental escalation clauses, commonly between 10% and 12+% per annum. The rental income derived from these premises, once the mortgages were paid in full after five years, was not only enough for my wife and me, but enough for the whole family to retire on!

The bank would have liked us to extend the repayment period and suggested that we use the money to expand our business activities, which would have kept us indebted to them for many more years. Were they really taking care of our interests or their own? Notwithstanding, we continue to labor and enjoy good health by God's grace.

3. What about insurance?

I believe in maintaining a balance between faith and common sense. One should insure your health, goods and business against catastrophic events such as death (to provide for your family and business) and fire (to replace items lost), to name but a few.

In our company, we insure only against catastrophic events. We self-insure our equipment, computers and the like. This saves us tens of thousands in premiums every year and, at the same time, encourages everybody not to be reckless because "we are insured". For example, should a staff member leave his or her laptop inside the car instead of in the trunk or in checked airline luggage, they are held liable if it is stolen. This has created a culture of responsibility within our organization.

4.   Should one pay your debts before tithing?

This is a very important question and best answered by Randy Alcorn in his book, *Money, Possessions and Eternity*: "Why am I in debt in the first place? Is God responsible for my unwise or greedy decisions that may have put me there? And even if I've come into debt legitimately, isn't my first debt to God? Isn't the tithe a debt to God since he says that it belongs to him and not to me? If we obey God and make good our financial debt to him, he'll help us as we seek to pay off our debts to others. But I must not rob God to pay men." [6]

In his book, *What to do when you don't know what to do*, Dr. David Jeremiah contends that the Lord will ask the wealthy only two questions:

1.   How did you gain your wealth?
2.   How did you use your wealth? [7]

By now, I trust that you will realize the importance of a capped lifestyle by closing your circle, and the amazing effect this will have on your church, your family, your employees and the community at large. As we share God's gifts, His grace and His message with others, they in turn will thank and honor God for His provision.

Once you are debt free, continue investing in heaven! Give freely to your church, your employees, the Lord's work and the needy.

CHAPTER 9

BURNOUT

"Unless the Lord builds a house, the builders' work is useless. Unless the Lord protects a city, sentries do no good.
It is senseless for you to work so hard from early morning until late at night, fearing you will starve to death; for God wants his loved ones to get their proper rest."

(Psalm 127:1–2)

"Often we must go through a messy period of our lives in which all aspects of it are in disarray.
It is in these times that God builds a new structure ... " [1]

(Os Hillman)

The Cost of High Achievement

I never considered myself a candidate for burnout.

The psychologist Herbert Freudenberger first coined the term "burnout" in his book, Burnout: The High Cost of High Achievement. What it is and how to survive it. He defined "burnout" as "the extinction of motivation or incentive, especially where one's devotion to a cause or relationship fails to produce the desired results." [2]

I always attributed "burnout" to people who weren't able to organize their lives effectively and, in some sense, did not possess the strength I had. What I didn't realize was that it has nothing to do with how strong one is. In fact, unguarded strengths are double weaknesses. I never recognized that not sleeping enough, responding to e-mails while traveling at all hours of the night, filling my schedule with appointments, numerous visits by international guests and endless meetings and projects were all taking their toll.

Add to this list the stress of doing business within the context of fluctuating exchange rates, high interest rates, political uncertainty and financial distress, and you have a fatal cocktail for burnout, unless properly managed.

Although physically well, I was battling emotionally. I became aggressive and flew off the handle at anyone not doing things "my way". In addition, I became forgetful, and small errands suddenly turned into insurmountable problems. I started avoiding important decisions, and simple tasks were left unattended. My energy levels dropped during the afternoons and I went home at four just to "relax". I resented going to the office in the morning and merely wanted to bury my head in the sand.

I came to realize that all was not well, as my forgetfulness and anger reached embarrassing proportions. After meetings, I had no energy to finalize or implement the decisions made. I only slept for a few hours and the slightest noise or movement would disturb me, eventually resulting in insomnia.

I made an appointment to see a specialist physician and gave him an account of my symptoms. After a complete physical examination and various blood tests, he concluded that my stressful environment and insomnia resulted in low serotonin levels, which in turn caused the dreaded condition of "burnout".

I had to admit to myself that the years of constantly working under pressure with regard to Eduplex, the withdrawal of the sponsors during the final phase, senior management problems at the school, frequent international flights across the time line, the six groups of international visitors we attended to earlier in the year on a week-by-week basis (each with their own demands and expectations), as well as the launch of various new products, agents' conferences and finally, the pressure of the brittle economy and the uncertain future, all contributed to my stress.

I realized that my friend Gerrit was possibly also suffering from burnout. He too experienced many years of working under difficult conditions in the ministry, having had to change course, working on a new curriculum, facing reduced financial support due to the credit crisis, plus a host of other pressures beyond his control.

How many other people were suffering from this condition; devoid of motivation, and beyond caring? Excessive workloads, attending to e-mails and the endless interruptions of telephone and mobile calls, not to mention the non-negotiable deadlines and fitful nights of tossing and turning, invariably ensued in frustrations vented on others in the morning—often on those we love the most, our spouses.

According to *www.time-management-guide.com*[3], certain categories of people and professions are particularly susceptible to job burnout. Most often, these are people who are highly committed and motivated, who have high standards and an idealistic dedication to their jobs. This condition more commonly occurs in professions such as entrepreneurs, managers (in business, education, health care, and many other fields), teachers, social workers and athletes.

According to this website, it is important to understand the risks of burnout in your personal job situation. Once you have become a victim, it may not be easy to get things back on track. This condition does not disappear overnight. You may not be able to recover by yourself, and may need to make drastic changes in your attitude and lifestyle. It is far better preventing it now, than putting your life back together later.

Once you recognize the symptoms of burnout, it is best to act early to prevent an irreversible condition. My own condition developed gradually over a period of time and I was fortunate enough to have received the diagnosis in the early stages.

Being a perfectionist does no good either. Many children, with one or both parents being alcoholics, tend to be perfectionists (as I can testify). For the rest of our lives, we try and make up for the mistakes of our parents and tend to over-perform.

In an e-devotional, Adrian Rodgers of Love Worth Finding Ministries says the following about perfectionism: "Your performance doesn't make you any more or less in God's eyes. If you think that God is going to accept you on the basis of your quiet time, your Bible study, or your service, you will fall into a trap of never knowing if you've done enough. You'll never truly feel accepted. Perfectionism is a thief. It promises rewards, but it steals joy and steals satisfaction. Why? Because perfectionism is an unattainable goal. If you are a perfectionist, you have set an impossible goal for yourself and therefore you will be constantly faced with frustration and failure. You are forgiven in Christ. You are righteous in Christ." [4]

Are you a perfectionist? Ask the Holy Spirit to free you from the fear of failure. Then make a conscious decision to be less than perfect and still be loved by God. I made that decision and I still remind myself of this resolution every day. Moreover, I strive to manage challenges, rather than people.

Symptoms of Burnout

My earliest symptoms were sleeplessness and frequent headaches. Initially, I surmised that the headaches were caused by my food allergies. However, avoiding the culprit foods did not help either. In addition, regular international flights over the time line impacted on my sleeping pattern.

I attributed my muscle and joint aches to my gym exercising routine and a possible allergy to red wine. I struggled to keep my weight stable and caught the flu virus every two to three months, from which it took me weeks to recover. My gym routine was interrupted because of this, which in turn caused more frustration. As soon as I started feeling better, I trained twice as hard to make up for lost time, only to fall ill again—a vicious cycle.

I experienced some scary spells of depression and Anita complained about my negative attitude, my anger and criticism of her and everybody else. Management meetings became a nightmare, as I aggressively asked questions out of frustration, and criticized systems and people—not contributing positively to our company or our management team.

I forgot what was said in previous meetings, which aggravated the situation, and I became convinced that my staff members were ganging up on me. This ultimately damaged my testimony as a Christian, as my "talk" was not reflected in my "walk". I realized that I was taking my eyes off the Lord and depending on my own strength, while trying to manage people rather than problems. To add insult to injury, I was burdened with guilt because of my anger. This was not the way to walk in God's will.

The Bible cautions, "... for when you are angry you give a mighty foothold to the devil ... Stop being mean, bad-tempered and angry. Quarreling, harsh words, and dislike of others should have no place in your lives" (Ephesians 4:27 and 31).

In his book, *The Greatest Thing in the World—Walking in Love*, author Henry Drummond says, "No form of vice, not worldliness, not greed of gold, not drunkenness itself, does more to unchristianize society than evil temper. For embittering life, for breaking up communities, for destroying the most sacred relationships, for devastating homes, for withering up men and women, for taking the bloom off childhood, in short, for sheer gratuitous misery-producing power this influence stands alone." [5]

I recognized that my anger resulted from burnout and that it was a direct consequence of the imbalance which gradually crept into my life. By increasingly trusting in my own abilities, I allowed a situation to develop that was not to the glory of God.

In his book, *Margin*, Richard A Swenson (MD) explains that the greatest emotional stressors are frustration and anger. "These block our ability to use stress in a positive manner and virtually assure painful and destructive results at some level." [6]

For me, everything had to happen "now"—probably retraceable to my days as a pharmacist when prescriptions had to be filled out immediately. When things did not happen instantly, it led to frustration, anger and criticism and I frequently asked out loud, "Am I the only one working in this company?" Of course this was not true.

Swenson describes "burnout" as follows: "Next time you fry bacon, leave one strip in the pan for an extra fifteen minutes. Then pick it up and look it over. This shriveled, charred, stiffened strip is analogous to what a person experiences in burnout." [7]

According to Swenson, some of the symptoms and attitudes of burnout include exhaustion, depression, irritability, paranoia, withdrawal, multiple psychosomatic illnesses, etc. "Avoiding all stress," he says, "is not an alternative to our overloaded condition. Those who have *no* stress in their lives—no novelty, no challenge, no change—are as miserable as those who have too much." [8]

The Cure

The cure, it seems, lies in balance or "margin", as Swenson calls it: "Margin is the gap between rest and exhaustion, the space between breathing freely and suffocating. It is the leeway we once had between ourselves and our limits. Margin is the opposite of overload. If we are overloaded we have no margin, or we have negative margin. If, however, we are careful to avoid overloading, margin reappears. Most people are not quite sure when they pass from margin to overload. Threshold points are not easily measureable and are also different for different people in different circumstances. We don't want to be underachievers (Heaven forbid!), so we fill our schedules uncritically. Options are as attractive as they are numerous, and we overbook.

"If we were equipped with a flashing light to indicate '100 percent full,' we could better gauge our capacities. But we don't have such an indicator light, and we don't know when we have overextended until we feel the pain. As a result, many people commit to a 120-percent life and wonder why the burden feels so heavy. It is rare to see a life prescheduled to only 80 percent, leaving a margin for responding to the unexpected that God sends our way." [9]

Once I was diagnosed with burnout, it was a tremendous relief. I wasn't suffering from Alzheimer's disease or losing my sanity. This was a condition that could be cured, provided I got help and made some immediate lifestyle and mental adjustments. I realized that "margin" was sadly lacking in my life and that it was all self-inflicted.

One of the biggest contributing factors to burnout is insomnia. Sleeplessness results in low serotonin levels, which in turn causes burnout. Relaxing before one goes to bed, and sleeping well, are important stimulants for the formation of serotonin and important ingredients for the eventual cure of burnout.

After my diagnosis, we were fortunate enough to go on vacation for 10 days, together with some very close friends. I was put onto medication for six months to enhance my low serotonin levels and improve my sleeping patterns. Within weeks, I felt like a new man. The aggression was gone and I became my "old self" again. I also began a course of antioxidants containing high doses of Vitamin A, B, C, D and E to boost energy and concentration levels.

Changing one's lifestyle is very important to prevent future bouts of burnout. For type A personalities like mine (often called "control freaks"), it is vital. A very close Christian friend said that after his burnout, he had to learn the following:

- There are other competent people in one's organization.
- We do not always have to be in control—things can be less than perfect.
- We need to trust people and delegate responsibilities. (However, we still have to exercise some control, as delegating without checking equates to abdication!)

- There is something like servant leadership and we should serve others by also giving them the opportunity to grow and develop under our guidance.
- We need to think before we speak, especially if we are under pressure.
- We have to be *very careful* not to seek stress-relief in alcohol.
- We need to exercise the whole person, i.e. mind, body and soul.

Our short vacation in the African bush was just what the doctor ordered. On returning to the office, I immediately started creating "margin" by managing my time better, delegating responsibilities, trusting my management and staff, allowing more time between appointments, taking time off and organizing my desk by getting rid of all the clutter.

By creating more "margin" in my life, I once again had time for my staff and friends in need of advice, assistance and fellowship. Once I allowed for interruptions in my daily schedule by not jam-packing my diary with appointments from one hour to the next, it was interesting to see how the number of people asking for advice and help increased. Now I had time to listen, offer advice and guide them as a mentor, rather than trying to control everyone and everything.

I started sleeping approximately seven hours a night, a luxury that had eluded me for years. My serotonin levels increased significantly and I became a different and more relaxed person. Ephesians 5:15–17 deeply influenced me during this time: "So be careful how you act; these are difficult days. Don't be fools; be wise: make the most of every opportunity you have for doing good. Don't act thoughtlessly, but try to find out and do whatever the Lord wants you to."

Doing simple things first, such as tidying my desk and my study at home, lifted my spirits. I had time to listen to the ideas of my managers and even express appreciation for what they were doing, rather than insisting on my own way. Delegating some of my workload added support, and by implementing some basic time management techniques, I regained "margin" and balance in my life.

Anita was overjoyed to have her best friend back. This was a wonderful compliment to me—a compliment I am sure any man would like to hear.

Balancing my professional and family life became a priority once more. Leaving the office that extra 30 or 60 minutes earlier afforded me some time alone at home, which made a remarkable difference.

I also guarded against slipping back into my old "negative margin" ways by trying to please everyone. I needed to delegate, ask for help and make time to relax. I needed to create "positive margin" in my life by becoming more discerning about that which was from "self" and that which was from God. I slowed down in the gym, rather than trying to increase my speed on the treadmill from one month to the next, comparing times, distances and calories. And I listened to sound advice from my son, "Dad, why don't you just run without a watch and enjoy it?"

Finding Peace

A few years ago, I visited our offices in Ghana. After spending a week there, I was ready to go home. On arriving at the airport, I was informed that the plane had been delayed and that departure was scheduled for the following evening. I was disappointed and upset. The next morning, during my quiet time, I shared my feelings of frustration and anger with the Lord, asking Him why this was necessary. The answer came via the Word: "The fruit of righteousness will be peace; the effect of righteousness will be quietness and confidence forever" (Isaiah 32:17 NIV).

The devotional reading was from *God Calling*: "My Peace it is which gives quietness and assurance for ever. My Peace that flows as some calm river through the dry land of life. That causes the trees and flowers of life to spring forth and to yield abundantly. Success is the result of work done in peace. Only so can work yield its increase. Let there be no hurry in your plans. You live not in time but in Eternity. It is in the Unseen that your life-future is being planned.

"Abide in Me, and I in you, so shall you bring forth much fruit. Be calm, assured, at rest. Love, not rush. Peace, not unrest. Nothing fitful. All effectual. Sown in Prayer, watered by Trust, bearing flower and fruit in Joy. I love you." [10]

The sentence that struck me was, *"You live not in time but in Eternity."* The Lord delayed a flight for 24 hours to teach me this simple truth. It had a profound impact on my spiritual life. The peace I subsequently experienced in dealing with business challenges was remarkable. I wish I could say that this state of mind continued, but unfortunately, after three months, I was back to my old ways of dealing with problems in my own strength. 18 months later I begged the Lord to restore the peace I had lost. Since then, I have been dealing with problems in a different way by changing that which I can, and accepting the things I cannot change.

Despite suffering from burnout, by the grace of God I never neglected my quiet time. In fact, I pressed even harder into the Lord and His Word as I realized how desperately I needed Him in my life. The patience, love and compassion I experienced from my family and the Lord during this "messy" time in my life sustained me enormously.

Now, whenever I feel irritated, I regard it as a red light on the dashboard of my life, telling me that something is faulty and that I simply have to stop and mend whatever is in need of repair. Often I pick up speed again, taking my eyes off the Lord, trusting in my own capabilities.

By slowing down and putting my complete trust in the Lord, fear about the future disappears and peace and calm, sleep and balance return.

CHAPTER 10

FRIENDSHIP

"I demand that you love each other as much as I love you. And here is how to measure it—the greatest love is shown when a person lays down his life for his friends; and you are my friends if you obey me."

(John 15:12–14)

Special Relationships

"You are my best friend!"

How many times have you heard or said these words and how often have you given thought to its meaning? How many friends, really intimate friends, do you have in a lifetime?

I know many people, but very few of them are friends. And only a very small number are intimate friends, friends I can count on in times of adversity. This kind of mutual friendship is not established overnight, but is cultivated over many years.

Not one of us is perfect and we all have some attributes that irritate others. I have come to realize that unless I accept my friends as they are, I will not have any friends at all. Accepting one another as we are, like Christ accepted us, is key to building lasting relationships. My friends accept my quirks and many faults, and therefore I should accept theirs unconditionally.

Gerrit and I have a very special relationship that dates back to 1977, prior to us getting to know Jesus as our Savior. At that stage, it was based on our mutual love for "life in the fast lane". After our conversion, it changed to a deeper relationship centered in Christ. Over the years, our loyalty towards one another cemented our relationship, despite various little disagreements, such as our country's politics. Gerrit has always been more liberal, whereas I tend to be more conservative. We have often had heated arguments, and yet, we have always respected one another's views.

Proverbs 27:17 (NIV) says, "As iron sharpens iron, so one man sharpens another." Sometimes we agreed to disagree and at other times, we would agree after giving it some thought. A good friendship is characterized by loyalty towards one another. Sticking together in difficult times, even if it calls for personal sacrifice, is what friendship is all about.

Both Gerrit and I truly believe that the kind of friendship we have cannot be cultivated outside of God's grace and years of praying together. It often implies a sacrifice, such as setting aside a week as often as possible (but at least once a year), to fellowship, to pray together and to seek God's guidance. We acquired this habit in 1985 and have since spent wonderful times of fellowship and fun together at our holiday home, as well as in the USA.

We have always prayed for our business and for Gerrit's ministry, and at times, the Lord led us to speak powerfully into one another's lives. It ranged from our relationships with our wives, our children, our staff, our finances, our personal time with the Lord, the future direction of our company and his ministry, our thoughts, our integrity in dealing with members of the opposite sex, etc. The Lord never failed to meet us as we sought Him—and at times, quite supernaturally.

I would like to share with you a recent event and the importance of not only praying about a problem, but also seeking to know what the Lord reveals through His Word, as well as the daily devotional books we use. In the mornings, Gerrit and I normally pray together and during the afternoons we enjoy our surrounds and what it has to offer.

During January 2009, we spent some time together in Telluride, Colorado. We prayed about the future of his ministry and he shared with me something that the Lord had laid on his heart: to minister the troops returning to the US from Iraq and Afghanistan. He told me that most of these soldiers suffered from post-traumatic stress disorder and that some had even tried to commit suicide, as they had been so traumatized by their battlefield experiences. Most of them felt that they had no future and no hope.

Gerrit was concerned that many of them had never received any spiritual support and therefore had no coping mechanisms or resistance to deal with the issues in their lives, let alone those in the lives of their families. We prayed together and asked the Lord to indicate whether Gerrit should get involved with the troops, or whether this would sidetrack him from his true calling, which was ministering people, mainly in Mexico and Cuba. Our prayer was followed by a reading from God Calling: "Help others. I ache to find a way into each life and heart …" [1] This gave Gerrit clarity about the way forward.

That same day, one of the soldiers Gerrit assisted phoned him after weeks of silence and asked to meet with him as soon as possible, as he once again felt very despondent. Pure coincidence? No. We believed God was "nudging" Gerrit in the right direction.

The next day, Gerrit expressed his concern regarding the way in which to minister these soldiers. After praying together, we once again read from *God Calling*: "Be a channel of helpfulness to others." [2] We also felt led to read Jeremiah 33:3 (NIV): "Call to me and I will answer you and tell you great and unsearchable things you do not know."

I was convinced that something new was about to happen in Gerrit's life. We went to lunch and after returning to our hotel, we felt the need to spend more time in prayer. We took Nehemiah's example as a strategy for Gerrit's approach in this new area of his ministry. In addition, the Lord led us to Isaiah 58:10: "... Help those in trouble!"

God's will and plan for Gerrit's life became clearer as we went along.

We once again asked God to confirm what Gerrit should do. The devotional reading that morning was from Os Hillman's *Today God is First*. Hillman quotes Exodus 14:15: "Tell the Israelites to move on." [3] Gerrit instantly knew that he had to move on, no matter what. We then read Psalm 34:19: "The good man does not escape all troubles—he has them too. But the Lord helps him in each and every one. Not one of his bones is broken."

He was encouraged to know that he had to start and, even though there would be challenges, the Lord would guide and help him. We are eagerly looking forward to see how this chapter in Gerrit's life will unfold. Supporting a friend in difficult times is what friendship is all about.

Accountability

Being accountable to other believers is an important part of every Christian's life. For the past 20 years, there has been an hour-long prayer meeting at my home every Thursday morning at five. My friends and I can testify to God's grace and miracles in each of our lives.

We all subscribe to the principles of being accountable to each other and "checking" on one another. During these meetings, one often notices that friends are also struggling with certain issues, and that no one is ultimately alone. James 5:16 has become our mantra: "Admit your faults to one another and pray for each other so that you may be healed. The earnest prayer of a righteous man has great power and wonderful results."

Being honest and open towards one another is only possible when there is an atmosphere of complete trust and confidentiality. We discuss our lives, business ventures, joys and challenges, and then pray for one another. We are a diverse group of people: I am a businessman, one friend is a financial advisor, another an engineer who bought a farm and started farming with Gerberas (a type of daisy) specifically to create jobs for unemployed people, the fourth is an engineer in the armaments industry manufacturing armored vehicles for export (many US troops' lives were saved by these vehicles in Iraq), and the fifth is a pastor from our congregation.

We check on each other's progress on a weekly basis, and at times we discuss particular challenges faced by one or more of the group. I struggled with anger for a long time and these friends would pray for me regularly. Through their prayers, I was often reminded that my anger could be the result of walking in a spirit of fear. Their prayers sustained me in difficult times and we often marveled at the Lord's answers to our prayers, sometimes on the same day of a particular prayer.

In *The Significance Principle—The Secret Behind High Performance People and Organizations,* the authors describe how a member of Dr. Charles Swindoll's accountability group would often challenge him about a particular area of life: "Over the years it became clear that his accountability group was one of the driving forces that kept both his ministry and his life on track. Of course, the challenges from his accountability group often hurt. But to this day, his personal circle of accountability friends help him to focus upon the type of husband, mentor, and leader that he wants to be. He knows that without personal accountability, he'd be in trouble." [4]

Respecting and trusting one another by sharing matters of confidentiality are key to a spiritually rewarding time as friends. A very dear friend of mine describes true friendship as follows: "Your name should always be safe in my mouth." What is shared among friends should stay between friends and we should not discuss others behind their backs.

Building Into One Another's Lives

Sharing an intimate friendship implies "building into one another's life". Can I call my friend a true friend when I have bad breath and he does not tell me about it? Can I call my friend a true friend when he sees that I am on the wrong track or walking into a trap and does not comment, warn or speak to me about it? Can I call my friend a true friend when he knows that I am following a path which runs straight to hell and does not warn me about my ways? Makes one think, doesn't it? How often do we have the courage to speak out, even if we have to risk our friendship?

I vividly remember the occasions when people had the courage to speak into my life. Although the first two instances did not involve friends, the words spoken had a profound impact on me. I participated in a swimming gala in the old Lourenço Marques (now known as Maputo in Mozambique) during my third year in high school. After the gala, I stood with a cigarette in one hand and a beer in the other, and the chaperone of our team came and stood right in front of me and said in Afrikaans (my home language), "Nico van der Merwe, vroeg ryp, vroeg vrot!" Directly translated, it means, "Nico van der Merwe, early to ripen, early to rot." I remember taking a puff of the cigarette and as I exhaled, said, "Guys, let's hit the strip clubs!"

Although it must have seemed as if her remark had no impact, it did indeed alter my thinking at that early age, as I vowed in my heart never to give that lady the satisfaction of seeing me "go rotten".

Shortly after my conversion in 1980, I wrote a Christmas letter to our clients and shared with them how the Lord had blessed us during the year. A client walked into the pharmacy and loudly quoted Matthew 7:21 in front of a number of people: "Not everyone who says to me 'Lord, Lord,' will enter the kingdom of heaven, but only he who does the will of my Father" (NIV). He promptly turned around and walked out. I was shocked and knew that he was referring to some issues in my life which did not line up with my confession of Jesus as my Lord and Savior. I had to re-align my life with the Word of God and realized that confessing my faith should not be mere lip service, but that I also had to be obedient to the Word.

How often do we underestimate the power of the spoken word? How often do we keep quiet when we should stand up for what is right, speak out and make our voices heard about the injustices around us? (Needless to say, we should first check the facts.)

On numerous occasions, my prayer partners had the courage to speak honestly into my life when they saw me taking a wrong turn. Because of our very close relationship, Gerrit has spoken seriously into my life, and I have done the same. These warnings produced life-changing results. During the time I was embroiled in an emotional snare with one of my co-workers, Gerrit and his wife Celeste spoke very directly to me on a number of occasions.

Eventually, I acknowledged and confessed the truth. They put our friendship on the line, because they loved both Anita and me. Some of my other friends also spoke to me, albeit somewhat apologetically, but none stood up to me in the way Gerrit and Celeste did—and for that I am most grateful. It saved my marriage and it saved my life.

How different would my life have turned out had it not been for these faithful, honest friends? Galatians 6:1–3 (NLT) says, "... if another Christian is overcome by some sin, you who are godly should gently and humbly help that person back onto the right path. And be careful not to fall into the same temptation yourself. Share each other's troubles and problems, and in this way obey the law of Christ. If you think you are too important to help someone in need, you are only fooling yourself. You are really a nobody."

Commitment

You can certainly not call yourself a good friend if you're not fully committed to the friendship. Sometimes, it may mean walking the proverbial extra mile, which may imply sharing your time, finances, or resources.

This brings me to the issue of commitment. There was a man who heard that his best friend was ill on another continent. The local doctors incorrectly diagnosed and treated the friend. The man arranged for his friend to fly home in business class and consult with the very best of physicians. He himself put aside three weeks to take care of his friend. He ensured that the friend was well on the road to recovery before he allowed him to return to his own home. He paid for all the medical treatment, including medication and surgery. In addition, he bought his friend some new clothes for the return trip to his wife and family ... truly a new man, ready to fulfill the mission the Lord had in store for him.

This story reminds me of the parable in Luke 10 where the Good Samaritan went the extra mile for a person who was a total stranger to him. How much more should we not walk the extra mile for our friends? How often have I seen people shy away from opening their wallets for a worthy cause, or to help a friend. I once shared with a close friend that we were experiencing cash-flow problems in our company due to the government not paying their accounts on time. I will never forget that he offered me an interest-free loan of US$250,000 to ease our tight liquidity situation. Although it was not necessary to make use of the loan, I greatly appreciated his offer and knew that he was a true friend. As the saying goes, "A friend in need is a friend indeed."

Proverbs 18:24 cautions, "There are 'friends' who pretend to be friends, but there is a friend who sticks closer than a brother."

People often caution others not to do business with family or friends. In all my years of being in business, I have embarked on projects with a number of close friends—and the majority had excellent results. Yes, some disappointed me, but that is life and those projects were in the absolute minority. In hindsight, I realized that those so-called "friends" were only intent on benefiting themselves.

My engineer prayer partner has worked on projects for us over the past 20 years, all with outstanding results. Likewise, my financial advisor friend has been my advisor for 20 years, and although we have differed on some investment issues, we could always agree to disagree and continue our friendship and business relationship. I always try to enter into business dealings with a clear mind and realistic expectations, especially when friends or family are involved.

I have a dentist friend who keeps reminding me to be careful not to imagine knowing what goes on in another person's mind, his wallet and his bed. He guarantees the outcome will nearly always be wrong. How true. Let us accept our friends unconditionally, with realistic expectations, and in love. Let us learn to put aside our own desires and reach out to them, especially in times of trouble.

And let us not forget the words of Jesus in John 15:12–14: "I demand that you love each other as much as I love you. And here is how to measure it—the greatest love is shown when a person lays down his life for his friends; and you are my friends if you obey me."

CHAPTER 11

THE OTHER SIDE OF THE COIN

" … not because of your own power or virtue
but because I, the Lord your God,
have glorified you."

(Isaiah 55:5b)

The Way of Life

Have you ever wondered how your life would have turned out had you not known the Lord? Or, if you are not a Christian, what would happen when you receive Jesus as your Savior and Lord?

I had such an experience and it was profound.

During my quiet time one Monday morning, I read from *Cheque Book of the Bank of Faith*. The author, C.H. Spurgeon, quotes Psalm 121:3: "He will not suffer thy foot to be moved," and then goes on to say, "The way of life is like travelling among the Alps. Along mountain paths one is constantly exposed to the slipping of the foot. Where the way is high the head is apt to swim, and then the feet soon slide: there are spots which are smooth as glass, and others that are rough with loose stones, and in either of these a fall is hard to avoid. He who throughout life is enabled to keep himself upright and to walk without stumbling has the best of reasons for gratitude." [1]

I read this passage without fully realizing the enormity of what was said, but the Lord was about to show me.

Our company's management team meets first thing every Monday morning. On that particular day, soon after the meeting, I received a call from a friend I last saw at my wedding, 37 years ago. To protect my friend's identity, I will call him "John". John asked whether he could come and see me urgently and we made an appointment for four o'clock that afternoon.

It would be apt to say that John was one of those people who had it all. John's father was a very successful architect in the city and the couple were regarded as model parents—soft-spoken, hospitable and very kind. In addition, John had the "gift of the gab". He seldom trained, and yet, every time we participated in a gala up to provincial level, John arrived a couple of days before the event, trained a few laps and chatted to the girls, only to reach second or third position in the competition. He was an attractive man with black wavy hair and a great personality. In addition, John's father gave him a Mini Cooper S—a status symbol in the sixties—to drive to school.

I, on the other hand, had to train hard, walk to school or catch a bus, and my dad was an alcoholic. Understandably, I envied John, his brother and his parents.

John promptly arrived at my office at four o'clock. I asked my personal assistant to direct him to my office rather than to one of the visitors' meeting rooms, as I was excited to see my friend again after 37 years. But the John I knew was not the person standing in front of me.

I stared in disbelief—and possibly longer than I should have. John had become a tramp. He stood there, reeking of urine, stale sweat and alcohol. Then the strangest thing happened: I saw myself standing in his shoes and John sitting behind my desk. I intuitively knew that the Lord was showing me "the other side of the coin", what I could have become had it not been for His grace …

Drugs, alcohol, nights on the street and time in prison all took their toll on John. He even showed me where he had been shot. I was curious to know what had happened in his life. He told me that after his father had passed away, a family trust was established. His brother, also an architect, stole the money and when he was caught, he committed suicide. John's mother died a "poor white" (as it was called in those days) and John, with a law degree, got hooked on alcohol and drugs, and never recovered.

Within minutes he said, "Let me show you what I can do!" He then did a head-stand in my office. I totally missed the point, as I was still in shock and more worried at what my staff would say if they walked past my office and saw a homeless person standing on his head (not bad for a guy of 57!). What John was trying to say was, "This is the one thing I can do that you can't!" He showed me his battered attaché case with a missing lock and an empty two-pint beer bottle—the total sum of all his possessions.

John asked for about US$6,00, as he owed the Nigerians (probably drug lords) that amount. If he did not pay his debt by that evening, they would kill him. I gave him US$24,00 and said, "John, please don't spend this on booze." He replied, "Thanks Nic, of course I'm going to have a few beers!" I smiled; at least he was honest.

Grace and Gratitude

On arriving home, I was distressed and in tears when I told Anita the story. Seeing the other side of the coin was not pleasant and made me realize how fortunate I was. I could easily have slipped and ended up the way John did. That evening, I re-read Spurgeon's commentary—and suddenly, it had a whole new meaning. I felt immense gratitude towards the Lord for helping me up during the many times my feet slipped and I stumbled.

Two days later, I read from Spurgeon's book again. He quotes Jeremiah 31:14: "My people shall be satisfied with my goodness, saith the Lord." He comments that very few people are ever satisfied with their lot. "Only sanctified souls," he says, "are satisfied souls. God Himself must both convert and content us." [2]

I learnt two major lessons in three days:

1. I need *to be grateful* to the Lord for His grace and for enabling me to have walked the road in His presence thus far; and
2. Apart from gratitude, I also need to be *satisfied*—satisfied with what I have and what I have achieved because of His grace: a life of contentment.

Two Scriptures will remain with me always:

- "So be careful. If you are thinking, 'Oh, I would never behave like that'— let this be a warning to you. For you too may fall into sin" (1 Corinthians 10:12); and

- " ... not because of your own power or virtue but because I, the Lord your God, have glorified you" (Isaiah 55:5b).

The Lord showed me the other side of the coin and what I would have been without Him ... nothing. For there, but by the grace of God, go I.

CHAPTER 12

THE KEY

"God looks down from heaven, searching among all mankind to see if there is a single one who does right and really seeks for God."

(Psalm 53:2)

"Are you a man or woman who is a seeker of God? The Lord delights in seeing those children of his who truly understand the meaning of life and why there is only one thing worth seeking—God Himself ... Do you have a consistent time of seeking Him in your life? Are you committed to developing that intimacy with your Lord that He so desires? If not, ask Him today to help you. This is the longing of His heart." [1]

(Os Hillman)

A Fulfilling Relationship with Christ

By now, I hope that you have come to realize that God can be trusted with *everything*—and that He knows infinitely more about being a businessman than we can ever dream of. I trust that you will also realize that there is something special, a key, which can unlock the door to a fulfilling relationship with Christ. Moreover, it is important to acknowledge that unless one has an *intimate relationship* with God, you cannot expect Him to lead and bless you in your day-to-day affairs.

The question arises: What is this key to a fruitful and meaningful relationship with the Lord? Let me try and answer this question in the simplest of terms. How does one cultivate a fruitful and meaningful relationship with one's spouse? By spending time together! No person can work day and night, participate in sport during your free time, sit in front of the television after an exhausting day, and then expect to have a meaningful relationship with your wife once you retire to the bedroom. We all know that this is not possible. Unless we spend *quality time* with our spouses and our children on a *regular basis,* we will not have the loving relationship most people yearn for.

Quality Time

The exact same principle applies to our relationship with the Lord. I can already hear the cries, "But you don't understand, I am already under so much stress and have so many time constraints and duties to perform. I simply don't have the time!" Forgive me for being frank, but unless you *make the time* and prioritize your daily activities, you will never have a fulfilling walk with the Lord. If you really want to know what God's purpose for your life is, then begin by spending time with Him, speaking to Him in prayer and delving into His Word—the Bible—for His answers. Ultimately, a person stands or falls by the quality of his quiet time.

I have spoken to many professional people, and everyone seems to have some excuse for not spending quality time with the Lord: "I pray in my car on my way to work" (hopefully with eyes wide open!); "I pray over my patients"; "I have my quiet time at work"; "I read through the Bible every year"; "I am too tired in the morning"; "I am not a morning person"; "I pray with friends"; and so forth …

Discipline

The bottom line is that it takes *discipline* to switch off the television and retire early; it takes *discipline* to get up early in the morning and spend time with the Lord; and it takes *discipline* to do it year in and year out. But one thing I can guarantee is that this sacrifice will change your life and it will not only change your life for the better, but also the way you think about and do business.

It is only by cultivating a regular and meaningful quiet time that one will experience results. No one can come into contact with the living God and not be changed for the better. The Bible says that if we want to know what God wants us to do, we need to ask Him and He will gladly tell us, but then we have to have a relationship with Him—and a relationship only grows over time (James 1:5–8).

I have often pondered God's words in Malachi 2:2 and the way in which they applied to my life: "… you haven't taken seriously the things that are most important to me." I made endless lists: obedience; looking after the poor; not oppressing my workers; tithing; feeding the hungry; keeping the Sabbath holy; being faithful to my wife; repenting; waiting on the Lord; trusting the Lord; etc. But somehow, I knew I was missing the point … The one truth, the most important of them all, eluded me until one morning.

Love

I found a little book on my desk, which I had never seen before. To this day, I don't know where it came from or who put it there: *The Greatest Thing in the World—Walking in Love* by Henry Drummond. The penny dropped and I instantly knew that the most important thing to the Lord is LOVE!

When speaking to His disciples at the Last Supper, Jesus said, "And so I am giving a new commandment to you now—love each other just as much as I love you. Your strong love for each other will prove to the world that you are my disciples" (John 13:34–35). Therefore, *love* should be the beginning and the end of a Christian's life. If I have love, everything, but everything else will fall into place: my relationship with Christ, with my spouse, my children, my friends, my employees, strangers—and even my "enemies".

But most importantly, loving Christ implies spending quality time with Him. How can I claim to be a Christian and love the Lord when I do not spend regular quality time in prayer and seeking God's will for my life?

You might respond, "Fine, you have made your point; tell me the secret, and give me the key!"

I again wish to stress that the "key" I'm about to share is not a formula for worldly success, money, power or fame. This is certainly not the purpose of my quiet time. In fact, some theologians may criticize my method as not being of "sound doctrine". Be that as it may, I can guarantee that if you implement these basic principles, your life will never be the same again; you *will* have a fulfilling and amazing walk with Christ.

I am sure there are many other ways to spend one's quiet time with God, but I have shared this method with numerous people over the years—and they have all testified that it has changed their lives. In fact, I only recently came to know that my God-fearing grandparents also used the same method. They prayed and then read from their Bible and daily devotional books. I trust that the basics of my quiet time will also come to mean much to you.

For your quiet time to bring about spiritual growth, you need the following:

1. A regular time and place of worship;
2. Prayer;
3. The Word of God and some daily devotional books (the latter being optional);

4. A receptive heart; and
5. Some form of record-keeping.

Step One: Prayer

God's Word declares, "For it's not *where* we worship that counts, but *how* we worship—is our worship spiritual and real? Do we have the Holy Spirit's help? For God is Spirit, and we must have his help to worship as we should" (John 4:21–23).

Prayer is one of the *two* most important aspects of quiet time. In fact, it is equally as important as reading the Word of God. If I pray only, how will I come to know God and His will for my life? Should I not be receptive to His Word, my decisions can be influenced by my own desires, circumstances and, of course, Satan, whose influence should never be underestimated.

Author of *What to do When you Don't Know What to Do*, Dr. David Jeremiah, states the four reasons why we should pray, based on James 5:13–20:

1. Verse 13: It is important to pray for emotional reasons—when trouble comes our way, we should pray for encouragement.
2. Verses 14–15: It is important to pray for physical reasons—when you are ill, ask the elders to come and pray for your healing.
3. Verses 15–16: It is important to pray for spiritual reasons—to confess our sins.
4. Verses 17–18: It is important to pray for national reasons. The prayer of a righteous man has great power and yields wonderful results. [2]

The author reminds us that James' final message to his scattered believing friends was this: God still answers prayer.[3] Remember, "The earnest prayer of a righteous man has great power and wonderful results" (James 5:16b).

Every Christian businessman can testify to the fact that there is always much to pray about. And it is comforting to know that God still answers prayer, both in good and bad times. My own prayers normally consist of the following (in order of priority):

- Praising the Lord for who and what He is (Matthew 6:9).
- Thanking the Lord for blessings, such as having saved us, for a loving wife, for peace in our home, a roof over our heads, food on the table, friends, family, security, etc.
- Praying for my family, friends, missions, church, community, country, etc.
- Expressing the hope that the Lord's message will spread rapidly and triumph wherever it goes (2 Thessalonians 3:1).
- Laying my own requests before the Lord and asking for His help and guidance in particular situations.
- Closing by praising and thanking the Lord for the outcome He will provide.

Prayer focuses me on the Lord and His love, grace and power. I am incredibly honest with the Lord, and at times, I even remind Him of His promises of years ago, which (in my impatience) I have not yet seen fulfilled.

Step Two: God's Word and Devotional Readings

The next very important aspect of quiet time is to *listen* to what the Lord says about that which you have asked or prayed about some moments before. The Bible is my first resource. It is also known as the Word of God—and I therefore read it with a sense of expectation.

In 2 Timothy 3:16–17, the apostle Paul explains the Word of God as follows: "The whole Bible was given to us by inspiration from God and is useful to teach us what is true and to make us realize what is wrong in our lives; it straightens us out and helps us do what is right. It is God's way of making us well prepared at every point, fully equipped to do good to everyone."

Furthermore, I read the message earmarked for that day in my daily devotional books. When something strikes me as being related to that which I have just prayed about, I underline it, think about it and then move on to the next book. You will find that the daily devotionals will bring some consistency to your quiet time. Try not to miss a day. The real blessing lies in reading the message pertaining to that particular day; not that of the day before or the day ahead—no, one day at a time.

Jesus Himself said that we should not be concerned about tomorrow and that we should live one day at a time: "So don't be anxious about tomorrow. God will take care of your tomorrow too. Live one day at a time" (Matthew 6:34). Stick to this routine and after 21 days it will be a habit!

At times, I am led to read the Bible first; at other times one of the devotional books. There is no set pattern, but again, the Bible as the Word of God should always stand central. It is uncanny how the devotional readings often support or confirm the biblical passages for a particular day. However, exercise the necessary caution not to become so busy with the "book of the month" that you do not study and meditate on the "Book of Life".

It is amazing how often God responds to my prayer almost immediately through His Word and the daily devotionals. At times, it seems unbelievable.

Step Three: A Receptive Heart

James emphasizes the importance of having a receptive heart: "But when you ask him, be sure that you really expect him to tell you, for a doubtful mind will be as unsettled as a wave of the sea that is driven and tossed by the wind; and every decision you then make will be uncertain, as you turn first this way, and then that. If you don't ask with faith, don't expect the Lord to give you any solid answer" (James 1:6–8).

Faith

Having faith in what the Lord instructs you to do is critically important. Read and receive the Word in your heart, make it your own and act accordingly.

Obedience

Once you have followed all these steps, the key is to be obedient. Making a decision without acting on it leads to nothing! Implement the decision in obedience, no matter how daunting the task may seem. If God instructs you to do something, then do it! He *will* make a way. Don't allow your own ideas, wishes, thoughts and fears to interfere with God's instruction(s). Ask Him for confirmation. He is always ready to assure you of His will. Should you still be hesitant, share your thoughts and the guidance you received with other Christians. God often uses fellow believers to assist His children.

Remember the account where the Lord led me (via 2 Kings 6:1–3) to purchase a property and I thought it was too good to be true? As I shared this with my family, my daughter said, "Wow Dad, isn't the Lord amazing!" This simple exclamation was all I needed as confirmation.

As mentioned before, I have been held accountable by many Christian friends, including Gerrit in the US. We have often used each other as "sounding boards" by discussing various issues over the phone, and then praying for each other. I have often requested prayer concerning various personal struggles, including sin in my life. Thus far, the prayers, advice, guidance and support of fellow Christian friends have proved to be invaluable. Being accountable to each other often culminates in clarity, especially when our minds are filled with doubt.

Proverbs 11:14b says, " ... with good counselors there is safety." This truth is endorsed by Proverbs 15:22: "Plans go wrong with too few counselors; many counselors bring success."

To have a trusting relationship with a fellow Christian (brother or sister) is essential in one's walk with the Lord. Sharing problems in a safe and confidential environment, knowing that we will be prayed for, clarifies the challenges we have to deal with and aids our decision-making. A word of caution: When looking for an accountability partner, find someone of the same sex. I have seen too many accountability sessions between opposite sexes leading to sin and a catastrophic ending. Always be aware that spiritual closeness can lead to sexual awareness. If a woman in need of guidance approaches me, I will see her once or twice before asking her to continue with another Christian sister. Be warned.

The following Scriptures underpin the importance of obedience:

- "But if anyone keeps looking steadily into God's law for free men, he will not only remember it but he will **do** what it says, and God will greatly bless him in everything he does" (James 1:25) [Emphasis mine].
- "You will be judged on whether or not you are **doing** what Christ wants you to. So watch what you **do** and what you think ..." (James 2:12) [Emphasis mine].
- "'Not all who sound religious are really godly people. They may refer to me as 'Lord,' but still won't get to heaven. For the decisive question is whether they **obey** my Father in heaven'" (Matthew 7:21) [Emphasis mine].
- "'All who listen to my instructions and **follow them** are wise, like a man who builds his house on solid rock'" (Matthew 7:24) [Emphasis mine].
- "'But if you stay in me and **obey my commands,** you may ask any request you like, and it will be granted!'" (John 15:7) [Emphasis mine].
- "So see to it that you **obey** him who is speaking to you" (Hebrews 12:25) [Emphasis mine].

I distinctly remember the Lord telling me one morning not to ignore the plight of widows and orphans. I replied that I did not know any widows and orphans. However, James 1:27 lingered in my mind: "The Christian who is pure and without fault, from God the Father's point of view, is the one who takes care of orphans and widows ..." Finally, I recalled that we had two widows in our employ and I immediately gave them each a small amount of money as the Lord had led me. They both thanked me gratefully, but then the one asked, "How did you know I needed the money? I have been asking God for some time to help me and you have just given me the exact amount I have been praying for!"

On another occasion, I had an appointment with my brother who was without a job. The morning before the appointment, the Holy Spirit led me to Isaiah 58:7: "Clothe those who are cold and don't hide from relatives who need your help." I immediately knew what to do.

The Lord spoke to me from the same verse during a freezing winter when it snowed—a rare phenomenon in our part of the world. I saw on television how people were living in the icy conditions in informal settlements near our city. I was convicted to immediately arrange 200 blankets for them. After distributing the blankets, I received a letter from an old lady who made me realize what it was all about. She wrote, "Today, I realized that God has not forgotten me." It was not about me! It was all about the honor and the glory of God. This lady had no one to turn to but God, and God answered her prayer by using one of His servants.

I mention these occurrences (and there are many more) not to impress you, but to highlight the importance of being obedient to the Lord. It involves more than asking and more than believing, but actually *doing* what the Lord requires of us. As you follow this path of obedience, you will experience God's richest blessings.

Patience

At times, you may feel that God is taking His time to respond to your prayers. Psalm 27:14 says, "Don't be impatient. Wait for the Lord, and he will come and save you! Be brave, stouthearted and courageous. Yes, wait and he will help you."

Author C.H. Spurgeon reminds us, "Wait! Wait! Let your waiting be on the Lord! He is worth waiting for. He never disappoints the waiting soul. While waiting, keep up your spirits. Expect a great deliverance, and be ready to praise God for it." [4]

Step Four: Record-keeping

As I read though the Bible and the daily devotionals, I highlight a verse or passage of particular importance. I make a note of the date and the problem or issue I have prayed about. My Bible is filled with Post-it notes and on some pages in my daily devotional books there are even four or five of these, as I update what I had prayed about (often years before) and how the Lord provided and/or changed my circumstances since then. It is uncanny how year after year similar problems tend to crop up. I am greatly encouraged by these notes and my faith is strengthened, as I observe how God intervened and provided solutions to problems of the past.

Had I not written these notes, especially after asking the Lord's guidance in a particular situation, I would easily have forgotten His provision. By keeping a record of how God interceded in the past, I can now look to Him in tough times, knowing that He will come to my rescue, as always. Often, I need only trust and wait—probably the most difficult thing to do for an A-type personality—while the Lord develops patience in me.

By now, you may very well ask whether there is a particular time of day to enjoy your quiet time. I have always been guided by the following Scriptures: "O LORD, be gracious to us; we long for you. Be our strength **every morning,** our salvation in time of distress" (Isaiah 33:2 NIV) [Emphasis mine]. In Psalm 5:3, David says, "**Each morning** I will look to you in heaven and lay my requests before you, praying earnestly" [Emphasis mine].

The footnote relating to Psalm 5:1–3 in the *Life Application Bible* reads that the secret of a close relationship with God is to pray to him earnestly *every morning*. It further states that regular communication is fundamental to any friendship and is certainly necessary for a strong relationship with God. We need to follow the example of the great men of the Bible and communicate with Him daily. They all spent time with the Lord early in the morning as they sought His face and laid their requests before Him. A regular time to pray and to read God's Word is the basis of a fruitful and meaningful relationship with Christ.

Anita and I rise at quarter past four in the mornings and have our quiet time for the best part of an hour. The only reason why we rise so early is because we have a gym session three times a week just after five. Does this require a sacrifice? Of course it does! It means early dinners, if we go out, and early to bed (latest around ten o'clock at night). We have separate quiet times, but we often wake up in the early hours of the morning and then spend time praying together.

When to Start?

Start now! Don't procrastinate! Within 21 days this routine will become a wonderful part of your life. I am convinced that God is able to speak to you through numerous other daily devotional books, or perhaps you prefer using the Bible only. Ultimately, it is about spending time with the Lord and studying His Word.

In my busy life, I do not always have time to study the Word in such depth as I would like to, and the daily devotionals have therefore proved to be of great assistance. It is imperative to enjoy your quiet time when there are no interruptions, no urgent things to attend to, and no distractions. Early in the morning works best for me; for someone else it may work best after the children have left for school; and for another during lunch. Do what works best for you. You will be amazed by the blessings that await you once you enjoy a regular quiet time.

If your diary is over-extended and there is "just no time", I suggest you read Dr. Richard A Swenson's book, *Margin*. The author explains how to restore emotional, physical, financial and time reserves to overloaded lives by creating "margin"—that space that once existed between yourself and your limits. "Margin" is time held in reserve for contingencies or unanticipated situations. This book helped me to say "no" and to restore some degree of calm to my life. Thanks to "margin", I now have time to listen to people, to encourage and help those in need, and most importantly, to spend quality time with the Lord.

The Ultimate Question

Now for the ultimate question: If I have not accepted Jesus as my personal Savior, will my quiet time be blessed? I am afraid not.

You may use your quiet time to get to know the Lord, but knowledge alone is not enough for salvation. Even the demons knew who Jesus was (Mark 3:11), but they refused to follow and obey Him. Unless you accept Jesus Christ as your personal Savior, the Holy Spirit will not open the Bible to your understanding (Luke 24:44–49).

"But," you might argue, "I just can't believe an ancient religious book that is two thousand years old and out of touch!" If you have any doubts about the credibility of the Bible, I suggest you read John Blanchard's book, *Why believe the Bible?*

If you do not know our Lord and Savior Jesus Christ, and would like to receive Him into your life, then do so now. The Bible teaches that if you confess with your mouth, "Jesus is Lord," and believe in your heart that God raised Him from the dead, you will be saved. Jeremiah 29:13 says, "You will find me when you seek me, if you look for me in earnest." If you truly trust Christ as your Savior and acknowledge him as your Lord, you can claim these promises as your own. Come to Jesus and to His Word with an open mind. Ask God to make His message clear to you and for you to respond as you should. You have nothing to lose and everything to gain.

To help you receive Christ into your life, start by praying: "Almighty God and Father of our Lord Jesus Christ, I am a sinner. Please forgive my sins. I receive Jesus as my Lord and Savior, and invite You into my life. I submit to Your authority today and every day of my life from now on. Please give me the necessary faith, wisdom and understanding to serve You to the best of my ability, as I ask this in the Name of your Son and my Savior, Jesus Christ. Amen."

Once you have taken this brave and life-changing step by receiving Christ into your life by faith, it is vital that you immediately start spending time with the Lord. Study the Bible and read your daily devotionals. Join a Bible-based church and participate in prayer meetings and other church activities that will sustain your faith.

May the Lord bless you as you seek His will for your life and your business. He is eagerly awaiting your opening of the door: "'Look! I have been standing at the door and I am constantly knocking. If anyone hears me calling him and opens the door, I will come in and fellowship with him and he with me'" (Revelation 3:20).

If you've enjoyed this book, I pray that you will come to know the Lord as I have, and that you will acknowledge that He knows *everything* about your life and your business. In fact, He wrote the rules.

If you have received Christ into your life as a result of reading this book, or if you have any comments or questions, I would love to hear from you. Write to me at: P. O. Box 11125, Queenswood 0121, South Africa, or e-mail me at nico@hass.co.za

NOTES & RECOMMENDED READING

CHAPTER 1

1. A.J. Russell (Editor), *God Calling* (Uhrichsville, Ohio: Barbour Publishing, Inc., 1953), 67–68.

CHAPTER 2

1. C.H. Spurgeon, *Cheque Book of the Bank of Faith* (Ross-shire, Scotland: Christian Focus Publications, 1996), 336.
2. A.J. Russell (Editor), *God Calling* (Uhrichsville, Ohio: Barbour Publishing, Inc., 1953), 130.

CHAPTER 3

1. Stephen R Covey, *The 8th Habit – From Effectiveness to Greatness* (New York: Simon & Schuster, Inc., 2004), 65.
2. Os Hillman, *Today God is First* (Shippensburg, PA: Destiny Image Publishers, 2000), 321–322.
3. Bonnie Harvey, *George Müller—Man of Faith* (Uhrichsville, Ohio: Barbour Publishing, Inc., 1998).
4. Bruce Wilkinson, *The Dream Giver* (Wellington, South Africa: Lux Verbi. BM, 2003), 96.
5. Os Hillman, *Today God is First* (Shippensburg, PA: Destiny Image Publishers, 2000), 308–309.

CHAPTER 4

1. C.H. Spurgeon, *Cheque Book of the Bank of Faith* (Ross-shire, Scotland: Christian Focus Publications, 1996), 141.

2. Ibid., 142.
3. Ibid., 143.
4. Os Hillman, *Today God is First* (Shippensburg, PA: Destiny Image Publishers, 2000), 335–336.
5. Ibid., 337–338.
6. Max Lucado, *Grace for the Moment* (Nashville, Tennessee: Thomas Nelson Inc., 2000), 352.
7. C.H. Spurgeon, *Cheque Book of the Bank of Faith* (Ross-shire, Scotland: Christian Focus Publications, 1996), 166.
8. Max Lucado, *Grace for the Moment* (Nashville, Tennessee: Thomas Nelson Inc., 2000), 187.
9. A.J. Russell (Editor), *God Calling* (Uhrichsville, Ohio: Barbour Publishing, Inc., 1953), 124.
10. Os Hillman, *Today God is First* (Shippensburg, PA: Destiny Image Publishers, 2000), 176–177.

CHAPTER 5

1. Rick Joyner, *The Call* (Charlotte, NC: MorningStar Publications, 1999), 107.
2. Os Hillman, *Today God is First* (Shippensburg, PA: Destiny Image Publishers, 2000), 128–129.
3. C.H. Spurgeon, *Cheque Book of the Bank of Faith* (Ross-shire, Scotland: Christian Focus Publications, 1996), 250.
4. A.J. Russell (Editor), *God Calling* (Uhrichsville, Ohio: Barbour Publishing, Inc., 1953), 237–238.

CHAPTER 6

1. R. Kent Hughes, *Disciplines of a Godly Man* (Wheaton, Illinois: Crossway Books, a division of Good News Publishers, 10th Anniversary Edition, 2001), 125–126.
2. C.H. Spurgeon, *Cheque Book of the Bank of Faith* (Ross-shire, Scotland: Christian Focus Publications, 1996), 229.

3. Os Hillman, *Today God is First* (Shippensburg, PA: Destiny Image Publishers, 2000), 128.
4. Ibid., 230.
5. Ibid., 280–281.
6. Max Lucado, *Grace for the Moment* (Nashville, Tennessee: Thomas Nelson Inc., 2000), 202.

CHAPTER 7

1. Lois Mowday Rabey, *The Snare* (Colorado Springs, Colorado: NavPress Publishing Group, 1988), back cover copy. Used by permission of OM Books. Www.ombooks.org
2. Ibid., 26–27.
3. John Piper, *Battling Unbelief* (Vereeniging, South Africa: Christian Art Publishers, 2008), 136.
4. A.J. Russell (Editor), *God Calling* (Uhrichsville, Ohio: Barbour Publishing, Inc., 1953), 188.
5. Max Lucado, *Grace for the Moment* (Nashville, Tennessee: Thomas Nelson Inc., 2000), 305.
6. Patrick M Morley, *The Man in the Mirror* (USA: Wolgemuth & Hyatt, Publishers, Inc., 1989), 131.
7. John Piper, *Battling Unbelief* (Vereeniging, South Africa: Christian Art Publishers, 2008), 92–93.
8. Ibid., 40.
9. Max Lucado, *Grace for the Moment* (Nashville, Tennessee: Thomas Nelson Inc., 2000), 201.

CHAPTER 8

1. Larry Burkett, *Debt-free Living* (Chicago: Moody Publishers/Crown Financial, 2010).
2. Randy Alcorn, *Money, Possessions and Eternity* (Carol Stream, Illinois: Tyndale House Publishers, Inc., 1989), 291.
3. Ibid., 297.

4. C.H. Spurgeon, *Cheque Book of the Bank of Faith* (Ross-shire, Scotland: Christian Focus Publications, 1996), 22.
5. Randy Alcorn, *Money, Possessions and Eternity* (Carol Stream, Illinois: Tyndale House Publishers, Inc., 1989), 301.
6. Ibid., 188.
7. Dr. David Jeremiah, *What to do when you don't know what to do* (Colorado Springs, USA: Cook Communications Ministries/David C Cook, 2009), 170. Used by permission of Cook Communications Ministries/David C Cook. Copyright 2009 David Jeremiah. All rights reserved. May not be reproduced in any way without publisher permission.

CHAPTER 9

1. Os Hillman, *Today God is First* (Shippensburg, PA: Destiny Image Publishers, 2000), 231.
2. http://www.infoplease.com/ipa/A0781755.html
3. www.time-management-guide.com
4. Adrian Rogers, Love Worth Finding Ministries, e-Devotional.
5. Henry Drummond, *The Greatest Thing in the World—Walking in Love*, (New Kensington, PA: Whitaker House, 1981), 31–32.
6. Richard A Swenson, *Margin* (Colorado Springs, Colorado: NavPress, 1992), 68. Used by permission of NavPress, all rights reserved. www.navpress.com
7. Ibid., 70.
8. Ibid., 70–71.
9. Ibid., 92.
10. A.J. Russell (Editor), *God Calling* (Uhrichsville, Ohio: Barbour Publishing, Inc., 1953), 179–180.

CHAPTER 10

1. A.J. Russell (Editor), *God Calling* (Uhrichsville, Ohio: Barbour Publishing, Inc., 1953), 22.

2. Ibid., 22.
3. Os Hillman, *Today God is First* (Shippensburg, PA: Destiny Image Publishers, 2000), 15.
4. Dr. Les Carter and Jim Underwood, *The Significance Principle* (Nashville, Tennessee: Broadman & Holman Publishers, 1998), 222. Used by permission of authors.

CHAPTER 11

1. C.H. Spurgeon, *Cheque Book of the Bank of Faith* (Ross-shire, Scotland: Christian Focus Publications, 1996), 315.
2. Ibid., 317.

CHAPTER 12

1. Os Hillman, *Today God is First* (Shippensburg, PA: Destiny Image Publishers, 2000), 192.
2. Dr. David Jeremiah, *What to do when you don't know what to do* (Colorado Springs, USA: Cook Communications Ministries/David C Cook, 2009), 200–213. Used by permission of Cook Communications Ministries/David C Cook. Copyright 2009 David Jeremiah. All rights reserved. May not be reproduced in any way without publisher permission.
3. Ibid., 216.
4. C.H. Spurgeon, *Cheque Book of the Bank of Faith* (Ross-shire, Scotland: Christian Focus Publications, 1996), 250.

Made in the USA
Charleston, SC
20 October 2010